For Rebekah, the best dinosaur princess I've ever met.

Before You Code: Validate your idea, plan your product and iterate your way to success
By Heather O'Neill and Jen Kramer

Publisher: Heather O'Neill

Developmental Editor: Deb Hardy

Editor/Production Editor: Meg Foley

Proofreader: Jim O'Neill

Book/eBook Design: Baremade Studio

Published by Pixels for Humans.

ISBN 978-1-7328906-3-3

Printed and bound in the United States of America

PIXELS *for* HUMANS

BEFORE YOU CODE

[VALIDATE YOUR IDEA,
PLAN YOUR PRODUCT, AND
ITERATE YOUR WAY TO SUCCESS

Heather O'Neill & Jen Kramer

FOREWORD BY SARAH DOODY

"Writing code doesn't matter if there's no strategy behind it."

-B. Cordelia Yu, 18F

Table of Contents

Foreword

BY SARAH DOODY

What if you could sell a product before you create it?

I'm serious. What if you could actually have people pay you before you invest your own time and money into building that product?

Imagine eliminating so much of the risk of entrepreneurship by quickly, yet thoroughly, working through a process that gets you tangible results, raving fans, and – of course – revenue.

I've done it, and it's not as hard as it sounds. And best of all, it doesn't have to take much longer than the method you're using now. You simply have to change the way you think about product development.

When most entrepreneurs start out, it goes something like this:

+ Have an idea

+ Buy domain name

+ Ask friends and family

+ Spend half a day researching competitors

+ Start researching where to hire computer programmers

+ Hire a developer with your own money

+ Get a version of your app back

+ Make tweak after tweak. Takes 7 times longer than you imagined

+ Plan your launch party/announcement

+ Launch

+ Crickets

Why does this happen? And why are so many entrepreneurs surprised when they launch their product, only to realize that people don't sign up for it? Or sign up, but don't come back? Or sign up, try to use it, and send a barrage of frustrated emails asking how to do things that were supposedly obvious?

Why do so many entrepreneurs fail?

They fall into the build trap. They skip over understanding the problem and go straight to coding and designing. And that's a recipe for trouble.

The build phase is addictive, just like sugar. The more you get, the more you want. You get addicted to the feeling of progress, so you keep building. All the back and forth with your developers and designers feels like work. And work must mean progress, right?

Wrong.

The trouble with jumping into the build phase is that you don't know if you're building the right thing.

Einstein said that if he only had one hour to solve a problem, he would spend 55 minutes focusing on the problem and only 5 minutes on the solution.

Here's the secret: if you want to create a product that people need, that people want, and that people will pay for, then you have to fall in love with their problems.

When you fall in love with a person, you want to know everything about them. You think about them constantly and learn everything you can. In the same way, to create a successful product you have to cultivate a deep understanding of the people your product serves. Your ability to know your customer better than your competition – better even than the customer knows themselves – is the single most greatest competitive advantage that you can have.

When you fall in love with people and their problems, then you'll never have to guess what feature should come next. You'll have an intimate understanding of where people are now, where they want to be in the future, and what is stopping them from getting there. And when you have clarity on those three things, then creating a solution for them is much clearer.

I know that this works. In the summer of 2017, I pre-launched a new product idea. Less than two weeks later, I had booked $3,300 in sales, without building a thing. Now a year later, that product generates five figures in revenue every month.

How did I do it? Well first, here's what I didn't do:

I didn't invest thousands of dollars in creating that product.

I didn't get married to my vision of what it could be 3 years from now.

I didn't build it, hoping they would come.

Instead, I focused on doing the very minimum necessary to get my potential customers the results they wanted.

The problem I spotted came as a flood of messages across email, Facebook, LinkedIn, Twitter, and Instagram from fellow User Experience (UX) Designers who were struggling to create their UX portfolio, asking for advice and support. Overwhelmed by the sheer number of these messages over several months, I decided to take action: were these requests a sign of a problem that I could solve?

First, I did some research to validate my suspicions. I sent out a survey, and quickly had 400 responses detailing the challenges people were facing when creating their portfolios. Problem confirmed ✔.

After that, I launched into a rapid cycle of "launch and learn" to validate my idea at each and every step. I identified where people were, where they wanted to be, and what was stopping them. Then, and only then, did I begin to imagine my solution.

I put all my energy and time into understanding the problem, and it made a huge difference in what I chose to create.

So what was the solution? My grand vision was a beautifully branded, on-demand online course, fostering a community of people pursuing their UX careers. But I didn't build it yet. I didn't record a single video. I didn't write a single lesson. I didn't purchase domain names.

The very first thing I did was send out an email to everyone who filled out my survey, inviting them to an online beta workshop for $39.

I hit send and waited.

Within a week, 85 people had PAID to attend the workshop. I actually had to shut down registration due to high demand – which meant that I also had a waiting list of people who wanted in on the next workshop!

If no one had purchased my workshop, then I would have packed up, without having wasted too much time and money on the idea. But people did purchase. And they loved it. What's more, people actually got HIRED. Less than a month after running that first workshop, one of my students landed her dream UX job.

I kept launching and learning, and the program has grown significantly. I get emails every week from people who tell me they got hired, or that they finally have the confidence to talk to interviewers about their work.

None of this would have happened if I had not spotted the opportunity in the first place. But having ideas is cheap – what matters is your ability to execute on them.

If you want to be an entrepreneur who creates a product that people want, need, and will pay for, you must throw the "build" mindset out the window. Instead, you must become obsessed with people and their problems. You must commit to a cycle of launch and learn. You must avoid at all costs the temptation to build too soon.

By prioritizing people and their problems, you'll spend less time guessing and wishing, and more time creating something that truly delivers what they need.

In the pages that follow, you will find an exact blueprint to help you stay laser-focused on everything that must be done BEFORE you build. It won't always be easy. But it's far easier when you can move forward with confidence, having validated that you're on the right track.

Good luck. I can't wait to hear about what you create.

Introduction

Snapchat. iPad. Trello. Basecamp. All of these products have something in common: their success in the market.

On the flip side, there are countless market failures: Google Wave, Twitter Music, Facebook Deals, Zune, Google Glass, Amazon Fire Phone, and Qwikster, to name just a few. And in between, there are thousands of apps in decline – think Foursquare, MySpace, Angry Birds, etc. – whose initial burst of success has tapered off as people move on to the next big thing.

As of today, there are over 2 million apps in the iTunes and Google Play app stores. More than 90% of them are zombie apps, unfindable by any means except searching directly by name. Websites and web-based products fare no better: With more than a billion web pages in existence, getting onto that first page of Google search results is no small feat. It's a crowded and unforgiving ecosystem where only the strong survive.

So how do you ensure that your digital product is successful?

First, you have to decide what *success* actually means. Product teams tend to think in terms of the features and functionality that they plan to ship. Get the features into the product in time for the release date, and boom goes the dynamite! #winning

However, we will argue that success goes beyond the features listed on a product landing page. Why are those features included in the first place? Does your target audience appreciate the work you put in? Did they even notice? Did traffic or downloads increase? Are you solving larger societal problems with your work, as many websites and apps try to do? And how do you measure this impact effectively and consistently?

Those are just some of the possible metrics for measuring the success of your work. That leads us to our definition: **A successful website or application is one that meets the goals of its owner.** Why did they create the product in the first place? What problem were they trying to solve – and did they solve it?

This broad definition means that the ugly website you built on MySpace in 2005 might be successful. You wanted to learn a little HTML, follow your favorite bands, and post a daily photo of your lunch. Did you do those things? Then you succeeded! The tiny bit of traffic you got from your friends and family was a bonus, on top of the goals that you set.

If you're reading this book, chances are your ambitions are a bit beyond that early MySpace website. You have a unorthodox idea that you want to grow into something successful, but you have no idea where to start. Or perhaps you've chosen a starting point: You're thinking about the perfect shade of blue for your logo, or a list of features or screens, or the best way to reach your customers. Your product is just beginning. If that describes you, you're in the right place.

In this book, we'll teach you how to go from 0 to 100 with purpose and intention, to achieve success while understanding what works and how to repeat it. But first, let's look at some examples of what makes, or hinders, success.

Personality vs. Usability

The website for Lings Cars (*www.lingscars.com*) looks like a chaotic mess. (Recognize any elements from your 2005 MySpace page?) The bright, busy background, flashing animated GIFs, numerous calls to action, and cluttered content all seem to indicate an unusable, unsuccessful site. Indeed, Jen's students often ask if the website is for real, and whether it generates any business at all. And yet...

Figure 1: Lings Cars website seems overwhelming at first glance.

In a 2016 interview, Ling Valentine, the company's owner, noted that for her target audience, the website works perfectly. Citing more than $106 million in revenue in 2015, Ling believes her success is because people want a real connection to a person with a personality, rather than a faceless, corporate car rental company. A closer look at her website shows that, despite the chaos, the design does point newcomers toward the place to start. There's no confusion about what the website is for; the messaging is literally all over the website. Ling's target audience loves the connection with the owner and her larger-than-life personality.

And this is important. Because while Ling breaks conventional rules about what constitutes "aesthetically pleasing" and even "usable" designs, she does so in a way that is consistent and powerful, to create a certain impact. A good analogy of how this works is with music. There are groups of notes that sound pleasant together, arranged in a scale. When you first start writing music, you stay within that scale, following common progressions that sound good. As you learn more about the way different notes sound together and how they can be used to achieve different goals and moods, you can break some of those rules. Adding in notes outside the scale or deviating from common progressions can enhance a piece of music when done well.

The same is true for building web products. Once you've learned and understood the rules and their purpose, you can start to break them intentionally to achieve your goals. In this respect, Ling is something of a modern-day Mozart — able to break the rules without needing to learn them first; her intuition for what conventions to follow and what ones to break has created a website that, despite initial reactions, is wildly successful. While it's technically possible for you to have the same success as Ling based on your own intuition, a much better bet is to follow a thorough process. This book will teach you the skills to achieve repeatable success.

The University of Advanced Technology website (UAT) has a much simpler design than Ling's Cars, with one main focal point, and seems to align with more conventional website patterns. Like Ling's Cars, UAT uses a scattered assortment of animated elements to attract attention. However, UAT's moving elements are part of the actual website navigation. They're not just decorative, which turns this interesting concept into a frustrating experience. The "ideas" floating around the person's head are in constant slow rotation, which means you have to wait for the one you want to come around, and click on it before it disappears to the back again. The bottom navigation items periodically do the wave, unprompted – as they are in the midst of doing in the photo – making it hard to accurately select one of those sections.

Figure 2: The UAT site seems simple but is actually frustrating to interact with.
Source: https://www.uat.edu/.

What is UAT trying to achieve with this website? Who uses it, and what do they want to know? It seems that UAT assumes everyone is a potential student, that they know everything about the university, and that they just need to review a specific degree program. UAT isn't a well-known brand, so it's likely that website visitors have some questions about what UAT is, whether it's a private or public institution, whether it's a for-profit or non-profit school, how long it's been in existence, and where it's located, to say the least. The home page does little to communicate any of this, nor does it indicate where one would go to get such information.

All of this is to say that simplicity and visual appeal aren't everything! Even though the UAT website is cleaner, simpler, prettier, and more "interactive" than the Ling's Cars website, the UAT website presents challenges for its visitors. It doesn't serve its users well, which means it doesn't do the job that its owners need it to do; therefore, it doesn't really succeed.

Trust and Goodwill

Mobile products can have their own challenges too. For example, the Home Depot mobile app forces you to choose a location and pressures you to create an account, all before you've done anything in the app.

I frequently buy things online from many places, including Home Depot; in my mind, my location shouldn't matter. I just want to browse and potentially buy some products on my phone. I also worry that I will be shown higher pricing because of my location, even if I am purchasing online. I don't trust the app, but it requires me to submit my location, or I can't proceed. Needless to say, I opted to uninstall and browsed to their mobile website instead.

The Home Depot mobile site is better, but it keeps prompting me to download the app (thanks but no thanks). While I'm glad that the Home Depot mobile site meets my needs, it's frustrating to have to browse there when I know an app exists. For heavy Home Depot shoppers, this can mean they either compromise and enter their zip code anyway or just buy less often from Home Depot due to the extra effort of getting access on mobile. Either way, Home Depot loses out on brand goodwill and sales; frustrated customers may find that they phase out their Home Depot shopping over time, and they may be more likely to check Lowe's or Amazon first – all because of a product decision that wasn't fully considered. And while these sales losses won't ruin Home Depot, for a smaller, newer product like yours, a mistake like this could mean the difference between success and failure.

Figure 3: Home Depot's mobile app requires a location for online shopping.

Figure 4: The Home Depot mobile site is better than the app but still disrupts a regular shopping process.

In all of these examples, one thing stands out: Intentional, well-rounded consideration makes for better, more successful design. And that's good news for you, because while there's no foolproof way to guarantee success, you can stack the deck in your favor with solid planning before you start building. This book contains some concrete actions that you can take to set yourself on the path to success, all without ever writing a line of code. We'll cover the following topics:

BUSINESS STRATEGY	To determine whether your product is going to succeed, you need to understand what your overall business strategy is, and then use that strategy to inform decisions about your product.
PROJECT PLANNING	Each set of features, goals, or changes is a project, or a concrete set of end points that the product team will work toward in a finite time period. Organizing your projects will save you from distractions and keep you focused on the end goal.
RESEARCH	Now that you know what you want to do and what your business needs, it's time to understand your different audiences through research.
PERSONAS	Gathering data on your audience isn't enough. You need to put that data into a useful, helpful format (personas) to keep your team honest and help you make smart design and workflow decisions.
BRANDING	Who are you going to be? Branding is all about perception, so it's important to build your brand intentionally rather than letting it happen by chance.
CONTENT	The words, images, icons, videos, language, and graphics you use need just as much consideration as the workflows and design of your product.

INFORMATION ARCHITECTURE (IA)	Answer the following questions: How do you structure a new product or website? What flows make sense? How should you organize your navigation? What should you include (or exclude)?
WIREFRAMES	Put it all together by sketching out some wireframes. No design knowledge needed – just grab a Sharpie and some blank paper.
USABILITY TESTING	How do you know if your decisions are the right ones? Test them with real or potential users.
ANALYTICS	Track patterns and measure your results with the hard numbers of your business.
RESULTS	The jury is in; you have feedback and data! Now it's time to analyze, prioritize, and make some changes.

So turn the page, and start on your path to planned success!

How to Use This Book and Workbook

With a title like *Before You Code*, you may be wondering, "Do I need to do everything in this book before I start development of my product?"

Honestly, no. And that's not our intention. We wrote this book because in our experience, the process of creating a new product or feature looks something like this:

IDEA   CODE   HOPE IT WORKS

Figure 5: Common process of creating a new product.

When it should really look more like this:

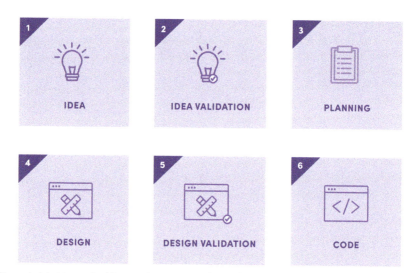

Figure 6: A better method for creating a new product or feature.

The best products, those that have repeatable, predictable success are ones that have a thorough process of research, validation and design supporting them. And that's what this book offers – the detailed pieces of the process that set you and your product up for success.

With that in mind, recognize where you are in your product journey and the overall process. We've tagged each chapter with the part of the process it focuses on, so you can know easily find the sections you need. After all, if you're adding a new feature to an existing product where a lot of upfront validation and research has already been done, that's very different than if you're just creating your product from scratch; you'll have more to do in the latter case, since it is all new.

It's also important to understand your org and your role within it. Are you part of a larger company or corporation? Are you the CEO or founder of a start-up? Are you a consultant who works with clients at various stages of their products? For this book we've mainly focused on startup founders' experiences creating a new product, though the methods and processes in this book can work for any of the above roles with some adaptation.

We've also designed a workbook with activities, essential takeaways, and key actions for each section – the workbook will help you take the principles of each chapter and apply it to your product, no matter your role or organization. It will also keep you on track for how all the pieces fit together, as many chapters build on each other. This way you and your team have a comprehensive document you can reference and update as your product is created and evolves.

Also remember that while we wrote this book in AN order, it's not THE order. That means you can do the activities for each chapter concurrently or out of written order. For example, some teams may want to start designing and coding WHILE validating an idea, because it's at a refinement stage. As long as you leave space for adjustments from that idea validation, you can do all your design validation after coding the whole thing or a prototype. The processes in this book aren't hard rules; they're guidelines of what to think about before and beyond coding out your next big thing and they have the flexibility to adjust to your process and needs.

So read this book and take smarter action – you'll have more success, and a better product.

IDEA

PLANNING

Understand Your Business

CHAPTER ONE

"The departments want to take our site and break it into more targeted microsites," Jen's potential client explained. "They aren't happy with the way the site is performing now, and they think they can do better on their own. Is this a smart strategy?"

To answer that question, Jen brought up the client's website for review, with an all-too-common result. The website was a jumble of products and services, with no immediate reason or pattern as to why one service was emphasized over another – at least it seemed that way. The images didn't help either; they were generic photos featuring happy, diverse people in business settings, giving Jen no insight into the context or industry being served. Jen's first impression was that this potential client must be in a completely different field than their actual industry.

Without any orientation about what the company did before Jen visited the website, she was unable to discern anything helpful about the company. Trying to analyze the website as a consultant, she was unable to figure out what the focus of the company was, who its target audience was, or what the website was trying to accomplish. As a visitor and potential customer, Jen had no idea if she was in the right place or if this website was actually for her.

She told the potential client, "You could spend lots of money developing microsites, but I doubt they'll produce better results for you. A better approach is to identify your organizational goals and your target audience. Then you need to decide how your website serves both of these. Once you define your goals and understand your target audience, you can restructure your website to maximize value and create meaningful content to support that service. Without doing the work of defining goals and audience, your messages will remain unfocused and unclear, no matter how many or few websites you have, and no matter what we do technically. Show how your organization helps users meet their goals. Telling them is never effective."

Jen's potential client wasn't fond of this answer. They thought the site and messaging were clear enough. It was their website, so, it made sense that it would be organized the way the company was organized. They thought that the organizational structure should be sufficient for translating the site to audience needs. Internal politics weighed heavily into the site structure and messaging too. It was easier to leave the website in its current form, rather than step on toes in order to rework it with the website's visitors as the focus. It was just as much Jen's job to help her potential client understand the process and its value as it was for Jen to understand and use the process herself.

Sound familiar? Many company stakeholders would rather talk about the correct shade of green for buttons and new cool feature ideas than discuss how the design and organization of their product supports the business principles and goals. However, without clear business purpose and strategy, your product has no foundation. You're building on shifting sands, and your product is bound to reflect that. Luckily, you're in the position to help any client, stakeholder or executive you're working with understand the value of connecting the product to the business direction.

In order for your product to be successful, consider the following essential information about the organization crucial to creating a user-centered product:

+ Mission and vision statements
+ Business goals
+ Competitors
+ Revenue streams
+ Value proposition

Mission and Vision Statements

A company's mission and vision statements are a litmus test for the organization's understanding of itself, and subsequent clarity of purpose. A company's mission and vision should directly reflect the specific audience, purpose, and values the company holds. However, many mission and vision statements are unclear, unfocused, out of date, or unrelated to what the organization is doing. Some companies don't even have mission or vision statements at all. Not having these statements is a strong indication that management is lacking some level of shared direction or purpose.

Mission statements describe the high level work a company does and why it matters. Good mission statements declare the goal and purpose of the organization in a succinct way. While they don't include every aspect of the business, they declare the main reason why the business exists. The best ones are current and regularly updated, and reflect the organization's values and activities. As shown in the example below, the Red Cross mission statement embodies all of these traits.

Vision statements describe what we strive to do and aspire to be. They offer insight into the implementation of the mission statement, explaining how the mission statement becomes reality. Becoming the premier dining destination in Boston is a mission. Offering high quality, creative food with outstanding service at an affordable price is the vision.

PRO TIP

While it's important for the company to have a defined mission and vision, they don't need to be front and center on the homepage. Instead consider how the message you do convey on the homepage speaks to and reflects those statements. If your team or CEO feel strongly about writing a letter about values, find an alternate place for that, like an about section or blog post.

Mission and vision statements are expertly implemented by the Red Cross, found at *www.redcross.org*:

> **Mission Statement**
> *The American Red Cross prevents and alleviates human suffering in the face of emergencies by mobilizing the power of volunteers and the generosity of donors.*
>
> **Vision Statement**
> *The American Red Cross, through its strong network of volunteers, donors and partners, is always there in times of need. We aspire to turn compassion into action so that...*
>
> *...all people affected by disaster across the country and around the world receive care, shelter and hope;*
> *...our communities are ready and prepared for disasters;*
> *...everyone in our country has access to safe, lifesaving blood and blood products;*
> *...all members of our armed services and their families find support and comfort whenever needed; and*
> *...in an emergency, there are always trained individuals nearby, ready to use their Red Cross skills to save lives.*

The balance of these two statements is perfect. Every item in the Red Cross vision statement ties back to their mission statement's core message, "preventing and alleviating human suffering."

The Red Cross carries this mission and vision throughout their website as well. Note how clearly the vision converts to the website navigation in Figure 1.1.

Figure 1.1: Navigation bar for www.redcross.org.

Mission and vision statements rarely translate to navigation as they do in this example. However, the mission and vision should inform the messaging on your website and in your products. Every page or interaction should reflect those statements; that reflection is a great check that you can do with your current product. Take a look at the page workflows, and interactions: Does each speak to the same core message? If not, how can you adjust it to be more aligned to your company's values and mission?

Business Goals

Product and business success is achieved when everyone on the team is aligned with and working towards the company's goals. Goal-centered alignment seems obvious, but the business goals can be elusive at even the most organized companies. For new companies or people without a well-defined purpose, these goals can be even more elusive. It's often easier to focus on landing the next sale or the next partnership than to think fully about the specific goals for the company direction beyond "make more money."

Why does this happen? Goals are hard, on multiple levels. First off, it's hard to make decisions intelligently about what comes next, especially if you are new to business. Setting goals can feel overwhelming and impossible if you've never done it before.

Even when considering a more established company, it can be difficult to achieve alignment across the leadership team about what the goals should be, especially if no one knows where to start. Too often decisions and direction are decided on a whim or based on someone's instincts or ideas. In those instances, the goals are known, at least somewhat, but they haven't been articulated in an obvious, clear way.

Sometimes goals exist, but are vague and unhelpful like "do better financially" or "get more people using our stuff." That's a good place to start, but what does that mean in a practical sense? How will we know when we've achieved success? What steps will we take to get there? Just like your mission and vision, your business goals need to be rooted in practicality.

Setting Business Goals

There are numerous ways to set goals for your business, depending on your style of working. We've briefly outlined two options here, but doing a quick online search for "setting business goals" will yield multiple other options if either of these doesn't resonate with you.

SWOT Analysis

SWOT stands for **S**trengths, **W**eaknesses, **O**pportunities, and **T**hreats. *SWOT analysis* is a method of identifying each of those factors for your business. By doing so, you'll be able to see areas where you need to improve or mitigate, as well as areas where you excel and potential new directions for your company. Strengths and weaknesses are the internal factors at your company – what things you do well and what areas reflect struggle or lack. Opportunities and threats represent the external factors that affect your company, both in your industry and in the world at large (the invention of the internet is one example of an opportunity that is industry agnostic).

To do a basic SWOT analysis, list out all the strengths, weaknesses, opportunities and threats for your company. This may feel like an obvious exercise, but as you dig in you'll uncover things you forgot about, and gain a shared perspective among your leadership team. Once the lists are fairly complete, prioritize the top items as goals. This method is a good one if you don't even have vague goals for your business. It also works well if you're trying to identify products and services that your competitors are missing.

Here's how this plays out. In the following table we've included a SWOT analyis of Pixels for Humans social media accounts. To set some marketing and social media goals, we can use the analysis to choose a few different directions. We could:

+ Maximize on the large size of our FB following, working to improve the content we share that's created by our team.

+ Choose to grow our LinkedIn following since the majority of our customers spend time there and it's a good place to reach them

+ Cultivate a twitter following and online relationships that supports our position as experts in the industry.

We may choose to do one or many or none of those, depending on the direction we want to take the company. The SWOT analysis helps us clearly see the options (and the tradeoffs).

PIXELS FOR HUMANS SOCIAL MEDIA SWOT ANALYSIS				
CHANNEL	**STRENGTHS**	**WEAKNESSES**	**OPPORTUNITIES**	**THREATS**
FACEBOOK	Strong following (15.7k). Thought provoking and appropriate content. 1 month of UX questions answered: great model for thought leadership content and solving problems for our audience.	Room for growth in producing and sharing articles written by Heather. Room for more SaaS-related content.	Room for growth in producing and sharing articles written by Heather. Room for more SaaS-related content.	Competitors with more diverse content.
LINKEDIN	With Pixels' team members having significant community, now is the time to prioritize the Company Page.	Low follower count, lack of engagement.	Demonstrate excellence, expertise and thought leadership in our industry directly where our target audience spends a majority of their time.	Necessity to always keep in mind the inappropriateness of common salesy content on this channel.
TWITTER	Diverse, appropriate and interesting content, good engagement when live-tweeting events/ hashtags.	Low follower count, lack of regular engagement.	Hub for thought leaders and several ways to reach out and build relationships with complementing thought leaders and we build community.	Twitter is high volume/ low quality and demands significant amount of time throughout the day to compete with other companies posting 20-40 tweets a day.

Figure 1.2: A SWOT analysis of the Pixels for Humans social media accounts.

SMART goals are goals that are **S**pecific, **M**easurable, **A**ttainable, **R**elevant, and **T**ime-specific. This method is a good choice if you have some vague goals that you'd like to make more tangible or actionable. The method follows the acronym: For each goal you are creating, confirm that it is:

+ **Specific:** Is it detailed or full of vague generalities?

+ **Measurable:** Can you determine whether you've achieved it?

+ **Attainable:** Is this possible to achieve (even if it might be a stretch)?

+ **Relevant:** Is it aligned with the direction your business is heading in, and with your mission and vision statements?

+ **Time-specific:** Is there urgency to focus on this goal now? When will you know if it's working or if you need to shift direction?

This method for goal setting is very common and very effective at turning vague ideas and goals into actionable goals that help your team focus.

Example:

Pixels for Humans would like to engage 4 SaaS companies in business growth consulting by the end of 2018.

These two methods can be combined for increased effectiveness, especially if you are new to goal setting. SWOT analysis can assist in identifying business areas that might be missed by you and your competitors, while SMART goals can help you turn those identified areas into executable goals. Regardless of method, it's important to create goals that keep you and your team moving forward; if your goals aren't doing that, it's time to rewrite them.

A Story of Three Goals

Business goals are important, but they aren't the only goals you'll encounter. Everyone one who uses or interacts with your product will have their own goals, and your product itself will have goals. Ultimately, every business needs three clearly defined sets of goals:

+ The organization's goals

+ The target audiences' goals

+ The product goals, including how it supports both the organization and the users

This may seem obvious, but many products fail to deliver on these principles. As we've already discussed, business owners tend to focus on details such as search engine optimization (SEO), app store placement, slick interfaces, hot technology, and beautiful designs, so they forget the overall reason that people are visiting their website or downloading their app in the first place. Those people have a goal, and they want to achieve that goal as quickly as possible.

The challenge of defining goals has been problem since 2001, when, at the beginning of Jen's career, her very first client wanted her to create a website for a large house for sale in southern Vermont.

At this time, the internet was still widely considered a novelty, so it was still a pleasant surprise to discover any company that had a website. Some real estate companies had started listing properties online, but most still kept large books in their lobbies, where potential buyers could come to flip through the listings.

The house in question was a 6-bedroom, 6-bathroom home located in southern Vermont, priced at $1.875 million. The current owner worked in home construction, and the home reflected his expertise. He remodeled a small house, updating it into a high-end home. His upgrades included a bocce ball court, an in-law apartment, a home gym, a waterfall in the back yard, a bed that slid outside to sleep under the stars, a gorgeous kitchen with 14 skylights, and so much more. It had been truly transformed into something special, and the price reflected that.

The challenge came from the disconnect between the local population and his target audience. The 2000 US Census listed the per capita income for the home's location in Windham County as $20,533 per year – not an audience looking for a million-dollar home. However, Windham County is located in the lower right corner of Vermont; it is within a half-day's drive of several metropolitan centers, including New York City, Boston, Montreal, and Albany. The opportunity was definitely there.

Let's consider the three sets of goals in the case of this home sale.

What Are the Organization's Goals?

In this case, the "organization" is the homeowner. He wants to sell his house, at a price that reflects its unique value, and without waiting more than 6 months for a buyer. Simple and clear!

Who Is the Target Audience, and What Are Their Goals?

Given that the house is selling for $1.875 million, the local population is not the target audience. The seller needs to find a homebuyer with deep pockets who is looking for a unique home in a rural area. There are some assumptions* we can make about this homebuyer:

+ **They probably don't live in Windham County, Vermont, currently.** To be able to afford an expensive home like this one, they need a substantial income. It's likely the right buyer will be found in one of the big cities nearby, or they're a wealthy international buyer. Advertising, therefore, will need to be far-reaching, beyond the local newspaper or the books in the local real estate offices. Putting the listing on the web is a logical, savvy way to reach this buyer, coupled with more traditional advertising in larger newspapers like the *New York Times*.

+ **They might be looking for a second (or third, or tenth) home, rather than a first home.** With the price point and location, it's unlikely that the buyer is in the market for their primary residence; the location is far enough away from nearby big cities to hinder regular commuting. This means that Jen's approach needed to be different from typical real estate website listings. With a second home, the potential buyer may be looking for a place to relax, that provides access to Vermont's year round outdoor activities: skiing, sledding, skating, ice fishing, hiking, and camping, Therefore, the website should emphasize the relaxing, vacation-like features of the house and nearby outdoor activities, with detailed information about driving distances and access, while de-emphasizing other features like school system ratings and neighborhood communities.

*Always validate assumptions whenever possible!

What Are the Goals Of This Product, And How Can It Support Both The Organization And the Users?

In this instance our product is the website. So we need to answer this question: Is the website responsible for selling this house? In other words, would someone view this website and decide to purchase immediately, without ever visiting the property? That happens occasionally, but it's rare, especially with a higher priced property.

More likely, a potential buyer needs enough information about the home and the area to make a decision to head to Vermont for a visit. Because it's about a half-day's drive from the nearest large cities in each direction, it's likely that the buyer would visit for the weekend, or at least overnight. This information, coupled with our understanding of potential buyers' perspectives and goals, tells us that our website goal is to generate strong interest with the right audience and offer them a way to take action, i.e., book a trip to visit the property and surrounding area.

Once Jen established these goals, she worked with her client to build a website that supported the goals. While the house took a few years to sell, due to the September 11, 2001 attacks and subsequent recession, the website played an essential role in finding the right buyer.

All of this demonstrates how the different goals at each level are important in understanding exactly how your product will serve its users and the organization overall. In this example, the website didn't need to serve every function of the organization, and it was targeted to a specific audience for maximum success. As you plan your product, whether a website or app, it's important to take your goals into account, starting with the business goals.

Competitors

Every organization has competitors. That's easy to understand if you're thinking about organizations that sell products, like fast food companies. When you think of McDonald's, it's easy to conjure up images of Burger King and Wendy's as obvious competitors. All three sell similar products and have similar business models; differences tend to come down to personal preferences and opinions.

However, some organizations' competitors are less obvious. Pine Street Inn, a non-profit that serves the homeless in the Boston area, is one such example: Their competitors are more difficult to identify. Do the homeless choose one organization over another based on the services provided? Is there even another option available for the homeless to choose? While these answers will lead us to one set of potential competitors, Pine Street Inn's main competitors are of a different type. In this case, Pine Street Inn competes for things like donations, government funding, and volunteer time and attention with organizations that are probably not even solving the same problem. To secure all of the resources and support it needs, Pine Street Inn needs to understand how it stacks up to a multitude of other services and organizations and how it can differentiate.

Whether your organization is more like McDonald's or Pine Street Inn, it has competitors. Some are direct and obvious, while others are subtler. Competitors might overlap for only one specific aspect of your organization, or they might be direct competition for everything you do.

In Chapter 3, we cover exactly how to do a competitive analysis, to make sense of your competitors, and learn from them.

Revenue Streams

When you're starting something new, especially if it's just a side project or small idea, it's easy to overlook your revenue stream. How this venture will make some money? Even if you are just hosting a small blog or website, you'll want to account for some source of income to cover hosting costs and your time in maintaining it. Understanding how money comes in, as well as the expenses that go out, is important when thinking about your product.

Sometimes revenue streams are obvious. Software as a service (SaaS) products charge for access or subscriptions. A fast food restaurant sells hamburgers. Colleges and universities charge tuition. The government receives funding through taxes. In all these examples, there's a clear, direct correlation between the offering and the funds.

However, there may be other revenue streams that are important and less obvious. Consider ads on a blog, affiliate links in your "recommended products" section, a virtual "tip" jar (like ko-fi.com), and bundled downloads. While these revenue streams are less common, they're still viable options, especially if your financial needs are minimal. As you grow, you'll want to consider what additional revenue models are going to best serve your company's needs.

Value Proposition

Along with the mission, vision, and goals, you'll need to define the company's value proposition. A *value proposition* is a statement that explains the benefit(s) that you company and product provide to those in your target audience. There are a variety of ways to write a value proposition and we've outlined three solid framework options to work from:

+ **Value proposition #1:** [Our product or service] helps [target audience] [solve current unsolved pain point or challenge]

> **Example:**
> Pixels for Humans helps tech companies scale their growth, ethically and sustainably.

+ Value proposition #2: [Target audience] [gets key value or transformation] from [our product or service]

> **Example:**
> SaaS startups can grow and still support their customers and larger communities using Pixels for Humans business consulting framework.

+ Value proposition #3: [Our product or service] [provides extra benefit or result] that you can't find anywhere else

> **Example:**
> Pixels for Humans provides a blueprint for responsible growth that you can't get from other SaaS business consultants.

It may take some finessing to find the right words, but using these structures to outline your company's value proposition will enable you to quickly share with people what you do and how it helps.

To arrive at the value proposition, you can review the results of your competitive analysis and ask some probing questions. Where are marketplace opportunities that your product can address? What do your users want that they're not currently getting?

Another great way to identify what is most valuable about your product is to ask your customers. Testimonials and customer feedback are great ways to pinpoint the value from your users' perspectives, in their words.

An example of a company with a great value proposition is MailChimp, one of many email newsletter service providers in the market. MailChimp differentiates itself by understanding that potential users aren't simply looking for features. Instead, customers want to know what problem the service is going to solve for them, i.e., the value proposition. In Figure 1.3, MailChimp's messaging speaks right to this value, right on the home page: *Send better email. Sell more stuff.*

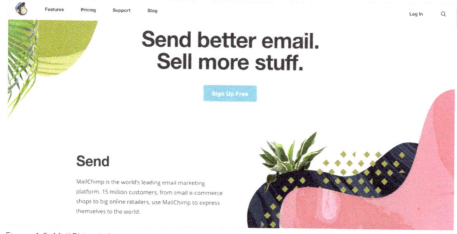

Figure 1.3: MailChimp's home page, www.mailchimp.com.

The rest of the MailChimp home page expands on this proposition, demonstrating the additional value that the software provides in achieving business growth and customer engagement.

The home page doesn't mention any pricing information or specific lists of features. MailChimp understands that their potential customers care most about the value they get – the problem that MailChimp will solve for them – rather than a detailed list of features or their pricing structure. With the value clearly communicated, visitors can navigate to subpages to learn about features and pricing. If MailChimp had led with pricing or feature information on the home page, it would have bolstered the assumption that all email services are the same, and they vary only on price.

Summary

A sound business strategy forms the basis of your product. Your strategy should address your business goals, your audience's goals, your organization's mission and vision statements, your competition, your anticipated revenue streams, and your value proposition. Before you do anything else, clearly identify your own organizational goals and understand your target audience's goals, needs, and challenges. Writing clear, relevant goals can be challenging, but the effort will pay off. Dig deep; look beyond the surface goals to find the real underlying goals.

Once you've established clear goals, use those goals to create your mission and vision statements. Well-crafted mission and vision statements clarify your organization's purpose and values, and provide a roadmap for a successful product. Finally, be sure to write a value proposition that enables you to communicate your product's benefits succinctly, compellingly, and consistently.

Put It in Action

A successful business starts with a clearly articulated mission and vision, and is supported by goals, clear revenue models that capitalize on the value proposition of your product and your company. To put this into action, define your own business details in the Business Canvas worksheet, found in the workbook. Once you've got that filled in, follow the prompts to see how your product fits in that picture of the business details you've just defined, using the Product to Business worksheet in the workbook. If there isn't alignment between your product and your business, determine whether your product, your business canvas or both should be adjusted.

Plan Your Projects

CHAPTER TWO

Once you understand the business, you can start making decisions about how to achieve the mission, vision, and goals you set, while delivering on your value proposition.

This means you need to move to execution planning. Execution planning takes into account the many moving parts of the business and breaks those parts up into projects.

Projects are the grouped, focused activities of an organization. Basically, they are the "what, when, and how" of executing on the business strategy – the overall plan for how a business will achieve its vision. In well-run organizations, projects are assigned to teams, with their own set of goals, objectives, and results. But where do these project goals, objectives, and results come from? In this chapter, you'll learn about the management side of planning and running your project.

Organizing Your Projects

The first step to a successful project is to clearly define it. A written project plan is a good way to do this. For freelancers and consultants, this might take the form of a proposal. If the product is being built internally, this plan is even more important, as it's easy to start any project based on an offhanded request from a stakeholder or manager, leading to poor project definition. Poor definitions lead to poor results, so it's worth taking the time to ask these questions before expensive development time has been wasted.

Here are the key questions to answer in your plan for each project:

+ What's the goal or purpose of this project?

+ Who is involved?

+ What roles will they play?

+ What are the risks and milestones in the project?

+ What other factors affect the project?

Your written project plan should also include sections that describe the logistics of the project, including listing tasks, defining how tasks will be managed, coordinating hand-offs between project personnel, and more. Project management software is widely available to help with this, and it's easily adapted to whatever plan you develop, so we recommend using a software tool to keep your team on plan. Don't be fooled though: just because you have project management software doesn't mean you're ready to manage a project. While software is useful with plan execution, it doesn't create the plan for you.

Let's look at the important sections of a project plan in more detail.

Project Purpose

As we saw with Jen's example in Chapter 1, every project needs a purpose. The project purpose is rarely the same as the business or product goal, but is instead in service of reaching those goals. Using your business, user, and product goals as a starting point, you should be able to determine the purpose of any project you're working on.

If the project in question has little relationship to your organization, target audience, or product goals, ask yourself and your team if now is the right time to work on this project, or if the project's purpose needs to be changed to bring it in line with these goals

List of Project Participants

Who will contribute to this project? It depends on the size of the project, of course. It could be as simple as one person – the person who has the idea and who will implement everything. However, more commonly, projects involve more than one participant.

Project teams often include:

+ Designers
+ Developers
+ Search engine optimization specialists
+ Content writers
+ Usability specialists
+ Project and product managers

These specialists may be all from one company, or they may be a mix of freelancers and internal team members.

Additionally, depending on your organizational structure, you may have members of management in your project mix, as well as folks from other teams including:

+ Some or all the C-suite or VP executives, or high-level managers/directors—anyone who's at a leadership or decision making level. These are your stakeholders.

+ A project sponsor: the person tasked with hiring or organizing the team to build the website or application, as well as tracking its progress, approving significant changes of direction or timeframe, and evaluating its success

+ The IT team

+ Marketing and social media teams

Depending on the size or importance of the project, there may be dozens of people involved, or there may be just a handful. Regardless of the team size, it's important to identify exactly who will be participating in the project, both by role and by specific contributions. Collect their contact information and note each person's role in the project, so everyone knows who to contact for various questions and how to get in touch with them.

PRO TIP

Identify Decision Makers

As you create your list of team members, it's important to recognize that some team members have more power than others. Essentially, some members of your team have the ability to change, redirect, or even cancel your project; veto everything you've done; or ask for something completely different from the agreed upon project scope. Frequently, this is one or more C-suite executives (like the CEO, CTO, or President), but it may also be someone else in the organization. If your organization is small, it may be you. By identifying those who have ultimate power in the direction of your project, you'll be able to ensure that they are consulted at every step, so there are no surprises and your project stays on track. This is especially important because decision makers rarely participate in projects on a daily basis. Keep them informed in project communications, even if they don't respond regularly and directly to your progress. And be sure to check in to make sure they are paying attention to the project and agree with the direction, by hosting in-person one-on-one check-ins.

A *deliverable* is a body of work you create and deliver, whether to yourself, to your company, or to your customers or clients. The ultimate deliverable is the product that you're building, but that product is often broken into many different smaller deliverables. For example, a typical website redesign project may include the following deliverables:

+ Acquisition of web hosting and installation of a content management system

+ Creation of site wireframes to finalize the structure, needed content, and site map

+ Creation of three different designs and two rounds of revisions for generating the site look and feel

+ Conversion of the finalized designs to code for installation on the site

+ Installation and configuration of additional site functionality (image gallery, blog, calendar, social media icons, etc.)

+ Creation of website content, including optimization of content for search engines

Notice that deliverables are broad and may encompass weeks or months of work. They also do not contain much detail, by design. Rather, they're meant to give a high-level overview of the results at each stage of the process.

Once you've identified your deliverables, you can outline the *activities* involved in your project. Activities are the individual tasks required to create a deliverable. It takes some time, for example, to create wireframes and designs for the website, especially including revisions. We can therefore break the step down further. For creating the visual designs, the project might specify the following activities:

+ Host a meeting or send out a questionnaire to identify your decision makers' preferences, the company's brand attributes, and a list of product elements, required features, sections, and functionality

+ Acquire and verify the final color palette, logo, fonts, relevant images, or ideas for appropriate images

+ Create designs in an appropriate format such as pen & paper, Sketch, Photoshop, HTML/CSS, or other agreed-upon tool

+ Post designs in a shared location that team members and decision makers can access

+ Collect feedback from appropriate personnel

Once you've created your list of deliverables and activities for a project, you've also created that project's *scope*. Scope simply means the list of all the items included as part of the project. To take it a step further, you may also note what is *out of scope*, or what should be excluded for the project. Sometimes out-of-scope items include additional deliverables or activities that haven't been vetted thoroughly or agreed upon by all decision makers. More often, items are out of scope because there isn't enough time in the schedule, money in the budget, or resource availability on the team to complete the additional items. By noting items as out of scope, you'll help your team stay focused on the actual needs of the project.

For example, you might include this scope description:

+ Team will identify 10 relevant stock images at 640 x 480 pixel dimension and at least 300dpi.

+ Out of scope: a photoshoot to create custom images.

Be Specific!

One of the most common clashes consultants have with clients is about project scope. Clients assume certain services are included in a contract, while consultants assume the client knows they are not. The more clearly you define what is in and out of scope on a given project, the less likely these clashes are to happen, and the happier your client will be with the outcome of the project.

Capture your scope information (deliverables, activities, and out-of-scope items) carefully in your project plan. Once you've drafted the scope, it's important to get sign-off from your decision makers. While you'll want to get your team aligned around the entire plan, ensuring that you're working on the correct scope for deliverables is crucial to the project's success.

The clearer you are, the clearer the communication becomes with your team, your decision makers, and anyone else involved in the project.

Milestones

A *milestone* is a point in time when a deliverable or a group of deliverables is complete. Milestones are the major dates that form the basis of your schedule in a project plan.

For example, the project plan might state that the visual design will be complete and approved by all necessary stakeholders 4 weeks from the project start. Notice that this milestone doesn't include all the activities and their individual due dates and times. You should schedule those details as well, of course, but milestones are only the due dates of major deliverables. While milestones should be communicated to clients, the myriad of smaller dates that make up deliverables are generally communicated to clients only on a specific request.

Generally, a project doesn't have many milestones. Milestone identification can vary from project to project, but these are the general guidelines:

+ **Tie milestones to your big deliverables.** In a website project, milestones might include visual design; completed site content, including videos and photos; a beta site; and a fully tested and debugged final website. You'll want to create milestones that make sense for your project, but the identified deliverables are a great place to start.

+ **Generally, milestones should occur every few weeks through the end of the project.** More frequent milestones can make the project feel too intense, while less frequent milestones decrease a sense of urgency. Your team needs the flexibility to account for unforeseen circumstances, without dragging the entire project out indefinitely.

Constraints

Every project includes constraints. These are any limits that might affect the deliverables. Some constraints are quite standard: Project completion deadlines, limited resource availability, and monetary limitations are all common constraints for most projects.

For companies with investors, additional constraints exist in the form of investor requirements (often outlined in your investor agreement) and input on the projects you work on. All companies and organizations must comply with federal, state, and local legal constraints, including HIPAA requirements for personal medical information, security requirements for capturing and storing credit card information, accessibility requirements, and more.

Your organization may also have less common constraints. If your target audience includes a majority of people who have limited internet access, that constraint needs to be factored into your design. If you're creating an e-commerce website, another constraint would be existing e-commerce patterns; your designs will need to reflect those patterns since that's what is familiar to your audience. Those types of constraints are called mental models and are discussed in more detail in Chapter 7.

Another example of a project-specific constraint is around usability testing. You may want to conduct user testing with people who fit your target audience profile. However, as we discuss in Chapter 9, recruiting some types of participants can be nearly impossible. In these cases, you would then be constrained to recruiting people ancillary to the target audience, and it's important to include that in your project plan.

In your plan, note any constraints that might limit your project. Think about money, time, resources, limitations in your knowledge, and any legal requirements that you may need to consider. By identifying your constraints up front, they are less likely to trip you up later.

Risks

All projects come with risks. By identifying risks to your project early you can preemptively consider how best to manage them, should the worst happen.

To identify the risks that might affect your project, consider risks along two axes of a matrix: The X-Axis represents the likeliness (unlikely to likely), and the Y-Axis represents the potential impact to the project (low to high). When considering your risks, consider both the external and the internal. An external risk is one coming from the outside: a bad economy, war, or stock market performance, for example. An internal risk is one that's within the project: for example, loss of funding, reduction of resources, or a change in management.

	UNLIKELY TO HAPPEN	LIKELY TO HAPPEN
LOW IMPACT	The train is delayed and meetings will be shifted to later in the day or held virtually.	Heather won't be able to connect to the client wifi during the meeting.
HIGH IMPACT	Dropbox goes out of business and all Pixels for Humans' files are deleted.	The project scope changes/is reduced due to funding issues.

Figure 2.1: A sample risk matrix from one of Heather's recent client projects.

All risks are worth considering, even briefly, but practically speaking, you can ignore many risks. Many risks are unlikely to materialize, lacking in significant impact, out of your control (i.e., external), or some combination of all three. If you spend time planning for these types of risks, you can end up stopping yourself before you've begun. For example, it's possible that an asteroid will hit the Earth, causing the end of life as we know it. That would have a huge impact on your project, but it's so unlikely it's not worth worrying about.

Some internal risks that are unlikely to materialize but that would have a high impact include significant changes to the team, especially the stakeholders. This happened to Heather once on a project; 80% of the way through the project, there was almost a complete change of team members. The new team wanted to prove their value and decided on a completely different direction for the project. However, they asked Heather and her team to redo the work with no addition to the budget, claiming the new requests were not significant scope changes. Of course they were, since the new scope had just been introduced; all the work had been done according to the old team's scope. Despite documentation and countless conversations, the new team wouldn't budge on their assertion that Heather's team should essentially work for free. The engagement ended shortly after that.

And that happens sometimes: Not every project is going to be a 100% win. By planning up front, you'll be ready to understand your own boundaries and compromises when these situations arise. Having clear documentation about decisions your team has made – including any key discussion points or rationale – will be your best defense to mitigate the impact. For unlikely but costly risks, determine the best practices you can follow to minimize the impact in a worst-case scenario.

Risks that are more likely but that have a low impact can be easily planned for at the start of your project. These might include minor schedule delays of 1 or 2 days, people taking vacation or an occasional sick day, or small fluctuations in project scope. For these types of risks, you should have a clear plan for how to react. You might build your milestones with a bit more space between them, for example, to give your team a buffer. Another thing to consider is what happens if someone is out unexpectedly for a longer period. Is someone else assigned to fill in that role, or does the project halt?

The risks that you should spend the most time carefully considering are those that are more likely and that would have a higher impact on your project. Typical examples include longer illnesses among key personnel, large scope changes, or schedule and feedback delays. It's also possible that funding and support for the project could be reduced or cut altogether, depending on the decision process of company leadership. Only you know which of these are likely risks at your organization, so identify these risks according to the specifics of your situation.

Occasionally, a client will request a product launch by a hard deadline; the product must be ready for a trade show, a TV commercial, or some other event. If this is the case, even minor scope changes and low risks with high likelihood can put the launch deadline in jeopardy. Be certain to communicate these constraints to the client upfront.

Your best preparation is to plan for these scenarios in advance, while you're clear-headed and not panicking. Write yourself (and your team, as needed) a few notes about these risks, along with plans for moving forward, or at least potential ideas to consider when reacting. Regardless of what risks you identify, set your team up for success in your project plan by adding some milestone buffers. It's always better to under-promise and over-deliver in your project. No stakeholder has ever complained that the project was good quality and delivered early!

Measuring Success

Fast-forward to the end of the project. Your team executed mostly according to plan, with a few hiccups along the way. Now you're ready to close out the project and evaluate its success. To do so, ask yourself and your team these questions: How will you know if you've succeeded? How will you measure the success of this project?

Remember the project purpose? That's the first point to review when measuring success: Did you achieve the purpose? If not, you'll want to figure out where you went wrong, and how you could move toward achieving it. It may also be the case that the purpose you were trying to achieve no longer makes sense; in this case it's best to refocus the energy of your team elsewhere.

It's likely that the purpose of your project is also tied to some product and business goals, which have associated metrics. Once the project is complete, review those metrics again: Have they improved at all? When comparing, be sure to map apples to apples in terms of metrics and timeframes. Don't compare a one month period to a three month period of results, or compare last year's bounce rate with this year's sales.

Remember that your metrics are only numbers; they can never tell you why something has changed. For example, back in 2000, Jen was working on a website redesign. Before the redesign, users were spending an average of 15 minutes on the site. After the redesign, the average time on site had decreased to 5 minutes. The client panicked: Had they done something wrong? Actually, they did a lot right! Rather than hunting through the website for information, website visitors were able to find the relevant information much faster than they could before, leading to a drop in time spent on the site. However, overall user satisfaction was increased, because the site was better organized.

To learn more about tracking different metrics, check out Chapter 10, Measure Your Impact.

Summary

A well-planned project addresses and supports all aspects of your business strategy. Your project plan should define the *what, when, who,* and *how* details, including deliverables, activities, scope, and milestones. Project plans also get all team members on the same page, and provide a blueprint for implementation.

Use your project plan to define key milestones for communicating with decision makers and stakeholders throughout the project to avoid miscommunication. Anticipate and communicate constraints and risks up front. Build in a reasonable amount of padding, and develop high-level contingency plans. If any aspect of your project doesn't go according to plan, you can avoid inefficient reactivity by instead responding according to your plan. Finally, be sure to define how you'll measure success at the end of the project and establish an existing baseline.

Put It in Action

Having a plan is essential to creating anything successfully, and building your product is no exception. Using your product description from the Product to Business worksheet, plan out as many details of your project as possible, so you can begin creating it quickly. Be sure to highlight anything you need to decide or discover, and fill in those blanks right away. Use this project plan as the basis for your project and as a reference as you continue to work through this book.

Conduct Your Research

CHAPTER THREE

Research covers a vast array of techniques that are all designed to uncover the behaviors, desires, and needs of potential customers and visitors. Research is important as it gives you real information from real people.

By conducting careful research, you know you're building something that fills a real need or solves a real problem. Research also helps to account for biases, assumptions, and unknowns, ensuring that your product is tailored to the audiences you are targeting. We'll cover two methods of research: customer interviews and competitor analyses. Resources for a few other techniques can be found in the appendix.

Customer Interviews

Customer interviews (also called ethnographic interviews or user interviews) are essentially long, one-sided conversations with individuals who are part of your audience. These conversations are structured to help you get key information about their behaviors, struggles, wants, and needs. However, for that information to be as accurate as possible, you need to put your participant at ease. You create that sense of ease through a conversation. Most often customer interviews are used at the start of a project, but they can be used later in the process, if you discover something essential you need to find out first hand.

Customer interviews are easy in their basic setup, but harder to master. These interviews are essential to understanding your customer and moving your product forward. Of course, you cannot just call up a customer on a whim and hope to get useful information. You must put together a cohesive interview plan that will allow you to get the information that will be most helpful for implementing a successful project.

As with many things, a successful round of customer interviews starts with a plan. Here are all the pieces involved:

Purpose

A customer interview is a conversation, but it's not a casual, happens-by-chance chat. The conversation has an intent behind it and you, as the interviewer, will want to get specific information; that information is your purpose. Because you cannot cover every topic in one conversation, you must define a clear purpose for each round of interviews. Being clear on your purpose upfront will allow you to structure your interview more easily and adlib more readily during the conversation. Be very specific in your purpose; know how these interviews will help you achieve your goals, so you are clear on what you really want to find out. This will help you conduct a valuable conversation. Here are some generalized examples of purpose for different customer interviews:

+ Validating assumptions

+ Discovering challenges with current workflows

+ Vetting a new idea

+ Understanding or defining audiences

Your purpose is likely to be more specific, but will have commonalities with or basis in some of the ideas listed above.

Once you have your purpose written, rewrite it several times. Yes, rewrite it. Your purpose functions not only as the backbone of the plan for your interviews, but also as a guide for you and your participant during the conversation itself. It's important to weave the purpose throughout the discussion to keep you and your participant focused and on track. However, you won't want to pause to reach for words or sound too rehearsed by saying the same exact thing every time you need to redirect the conversation back to the purpose. Instead, you'll want the conversation to continue to flow naturally by being able to vary your wording. By rewriting your purpose several times, and familiarizing yourself with each variation, you'll be able to carry the conversation more easily. Additionally, you'll be prepared to provide clarification and different explanations if your participant doesn't understand the purpose initially.

For example, if your purpose is to understand how your target audience manages their projects, you might end up with the following purpose variations:

+ Understand how project managers keep their projects organized

+ Discover the methods and tools used to manage projects

+ Learn what project managers do to keep projects on track

+ Identify the processes and software that people use to organize and run projects

+ See how people take a project from start to finish

As you can see, they all have the same core purpose and just vary on wording. As with any skill, the more often you practice this, the better you get at it.

Focus Audiences

Once you have a purpose, you can start to build out your interview plan by choosing your *focus audience* for this series of interviews. If you don't have a clear focus audience yet, you can skip to Chapter 4 to get started defining them as different personas. However, since personas work best when created from research, it may be worthwhile to start with a more general target audience and make the purpose of your research to discover your different audiences or personas.

If you already have clearly defined personas or audiences, ask yourself: Which personas are the most relevant and important for gathering the information you want to collect? Keep in mind that each persona has different goals, needs, and mental models as you consider the best fit.

If we were researching information on how people manage projects, one obvious persona would be people who are in a project management role. Another good option would be product managers, since they also often spend time managing multiple aspects of various projects. A less obvious option would be a freelance designer; if this person has multiple clients, they will need to manage each of their client projects.

Keep in mind that personas are not tied to job descriptions. You may have three personas within a given job title or a persona who spans multiple job titles. The idea is simply to identify, from the personas you create, who the primary focus of this particular series of customer interviews is.

PRO TIP

Researching New Personas

For initial persona creation, choosing a focus audience becomes a bit of a different situation. When you are trying to define your personas for the first time, you are working from more general assumptions about your audience, usually based on your own understanding. This means that you will focus on getting a broader range of participants (and more participants in total) to create your personas and validate your assumptions. We discuss how to use data collected from customer interviews to create personas in Chapter 4.

Explanations

This brief but essential section of your interview plan can seem almost trivial at first glance. Explanations are just descriptions of different terms, activities, or information that will come up over the course of your interview that may not be clear to the participant. A good example of an explanation in action is if you choose to do another activity, such as a card sort or task-completion activity during your interview, in addition to the conversation portion. You will want to explain to your participant what the activity is, what they need to do, and why it's helpful to you and, ultimately, to them.

Less obvious, but still necessary explanations include:

+ Information about recording the session

+ Different types of questions being asked (descriptive versus compare and contrast)

+ Any other people involved with the interview (such as observers)

Explanations, like variations of your purpose, are useful to consider in advance so you aren't left struggling for the right words in the moment.

For example, if you were interviewing people about their project management processes, you might ask each participant to take pre-created cards and sort them into the order of how they most prefer to organize their projects. When including this activity, you would also need to include an explanation of the activity, with any constraints (perhaps you want to limit the time they can spend deciding) or additional details (you may allow them to write their own ideas on cards, if they want a word or phrase that isn't on an existing card).

Any additions to the basic format of "interview," such as asking questions and listening to answers, will need additional explanations.

Questions

Finally, we get to the most important and biggest part of your customer interview plan: the questions you'll use as the basis for your conversation. Although this might seem straightforward, there are a few things to consider when writing your questions.

To start, you'll want to go back to your purpose and brainstorm questions that will help you achieve that purpose. The fact that you have spent time rephrasing your purpose should help you in creating your initial question set. Write down as many questions as you can think of. Once you've exhausted your ideas, go back through and organize the questions by combining or removing questions that are redundant or too similar.

During the brainstorming process, you may have written, "What tools do you use to organize your projects?" and later, "What is your go-to software for keeping projects on track?" Because those are essentially the same question, you can combine them into one question, either by rewriting or just choosing which one you believe will work best. You'll also want to edit your questions; be sure they are concise and open-ended. *Open-ended questions* are questions that have no set answer. They're open so the person answering can provide whatever answer makes sense to them.

Writing open-ended questions is important because you get the best, most informative and helpful information. With open-ended questions, your interviewees have to create their own answer; they can't just say yes or no. And that means you'll get their thoughts, in their own words. To write open-ended questions well, try to be as broad as possible, while still giving enough direction that someone can answer your question. In the example from the last paragraph, the first question that asks about "tools" is a better question to use, because it allows for a broader range of answers. With the second question, you'll only hear about software. This means if someone's main means is pen and paper, you won't find that out if your question is too specific.

As a part of creating questions, you'll want to consider the types of questions that are best suited to achieving your purpose. Most of your questions will be open-ended, descriptive questions. You may also want to include some structural questions (such as "Can you list at least 3 things you do every day to keep your projects on track?") and compare-and-contrast questions (such as "Describe the differences in your day when you spend time planning before a project starts versus just starting the project"). By creating a variety of questions, you can make sure you cover the crucial information that might not come up in a simple open-ended discussion.

Next, you'll want to note areas where you'll need to ad-lib follow-up questions on the fly; in the midst of an answer to one question, your participant may say something unknown or unexpected that you'll want to expand upon. Consider what topics you know the least about and what areas have the most opportunity for unexpected answers. These are the mostly likely questions where follow-up is required. For example, if you ask someone "What is your process for starting a new project?" you will listen for unexpected steps in the process, or tools and methods you are unfamiliar with.

To prepare for the interview in this example, write down your own understanding of how to start a new project, as well as all the tools and methodologies you are familiar with. Based on this list, you'll be much more equipped to notice something you don't know and need to follow up on.

Finally, you don't want to simply read from your questions list, so you'll need to create questions that you can easily remember and build upon during your conversation. There's no "interview police," so you can certainly look at your question list during the interview, but to keep it most conversational, it's best to have the questions (and the underlying purpose) in your mind.

The easiest questions to remember are the most basic, like "What is your process like?" and "Tell me about a typical day for you." These are broad, open questions that give your participant the opportunity to talk in depth about what they know. You can also use this to focus on a specific past experience, to help the participant answer successfully. "Tell me the steps you took to set up your latest project" is a great example of this. And because you did the prep work, you'll be able to identify the moments to dig deeper with follow-up questions.

Tips and Tricks for Conducting Successful Interviews

Most of us have been in awkward conversations before, when someone just keeps saying odd things or the conversation just falls flat. It can be uncomfortable and disconcerting. And, unfortunately, it's very possible for your customer interviews to end up feeling this way if you're not careful. Because of the nature of customer interviews, there will always be a level of awkwardness but these tips will help you maximize the information you collect, while keeping the conversation as comfortable as possible.

+ **Make the participant feel comfortable.** This is the most important thing you can do to ensure success. The more comfortable your participant feels, the more they will share about their own experience, rather than trying to answer what they think you want to hear. You and the participant know you are meeting for a reason. It's a natural human tendency to try to "achieve" a perceived goal; this impulse can actually hurt your ability to get the information you want. By keeping the participant at ease, you'll help them let go of their desire to "solve" your problem, and encourage them to just talk about their experience.

+ **Memorize your questions, purpose, and explanations**. The less time you have to spend thinking about "what comes next" or reading off of a list, the easier and more natural your conversation will feel.

+ **Express interest.** Practice active listening, and maintain active engagement in the conversation. This can feel a little unnatural at first, and you may end up coming across as too enthusiastic, but with practice you'll get a feel for actively expressing interest in a compelling way. Too many bland "uh-huhs" and your interview subject may feel like you're not listening.

It's also important to remain neutral, even as you express interest – so you're interested, but you're not telling them something is "right" and accidentally leading them down a path to get more confirmation. It's the difference between saying "Yeah, that's a great idea!" and "That's really interesting. Tell me more." The second response leaves space for the participant to talk about what's important to them, instead of trying to say what they think is important to you. It also means they won't worry they've said something "wrong" when you don't affirm their words.

+ **Express cultural ignorance.** Every industry has a culture: Think how Starbucks fans know the secret off-menu drinks or how government employees sound like they're reading random sets of Scrabble titles with so many acronyms. Because your product is a part of its world, you might already know a great deal about your participants and their contexts, experiences, and needs. However, to get the most out of your interview, it's best to act as though you know nothing at all. By giving your participant the opportunity to tell you things you "know," you'll be able to find out where your knowledge is inaccurate, and you'll pick up on nuances you may not have considered and additional information you did not know.

It's also important to consider actual world cultures; for example, what potential impact does your product have on Black people or in Muslim communities? What about for people who are English as a Second Language (ESL) or disabled? Each of those cultures has their own needs. In the same way as with industry cultures, be sure to express ignorance, even if you think you know. You'll learn so much more, and be able to update your understanding instead of working from stereotypes and assumptions.

+ **Restate what has been said and incorporate what you have heard.** These two tips might seem obvious, but it's surprising how often they are overlooked. Restating what has been said goes well with expressing interest; by doing so, you confirm what you have heard and give the participant the opportunity to verify your understanding or add and correct information. Incorporating what you have heard helps to move the conversation forward. It provides a good lead-in to additional questions in a simple, natural way. Both have the added value of making the participant feel heard and, ultimately, more comfortable.

+ **Pause.** Wait, what? Yes, pause. This may seem counter-intuitive, especially given the first tip of making the participant feel comfortable, but it's very effective for getting more information. If you give your participant space to think, instead of launching right into the next question, most often, they will add to their initial answer, giving you more valuable information. And be extra careful not to jump in with your own ideas. You're there to listen and learn, not to talk.

+ **Course correct.** Sometimes your participant ends up on a tangent or in a discussion that distracts from your purpose. In these moments, it's important to bring them back to the conversation you want to have. This can be done at a pause in the discussion or, if the participant is on a roll, by simply saying, "I'm sorry, but I'm going to interrupt you here since I have a few more things I want to discuss before we end our time here today." This way, you stick to your purpose but still make the participant feel comfortable.

Also be wary of participant questions. Often times, the participant will ask a question that's not appropriate for you to answer because it may bias the study, or influence their answers. Instead of answering, let them know that you can't answer that now but can share more about the project at the end of the interview.

Refocusing also works if you discover that some of your questions do not lead to the information you were hoping to get. While you can adjust your question list between interviews, you'll also want to salvage as much of the interview as possible in real time by refocusing yourself and your participant.

+ **Do practice interviews.** Even if you have time for only one practice interview, it's important to do it. Practice interviews let you catch any flaws in your test plan early, and give you an opportunity to practice your interview skills. This is essential if you are new to running interviews. You'll be surprised by what you can learn, even in a test run with coworkers who already have your shared knowledge.

Conducting a Competitor Analysis

One of the best things you can do when creating a new product (or updating an existing one) is an analysis of your competition. A *competitor analysis* provides an in-depth investigation into the ins and outs of your competition, from what they are and are not offering, to the perceptions and buzz around their brand identities, to their price structure and target audiences. This will help you consider how to position yourself in that market and fill gaps in what's being offered. No matter what industry you're in, you have competition, and you can learn a great deal from these competitors.

There are many ways to collect and analyze this information; indeed, some jobs and companies are solely dedicated to studying competitors and markets. For this book, however, we'll cover a basic (but effective) method for researching competitors and analyzing the information. This method is designed to be manageable for any level of experience and timeframe.

A competitor analysis will provide you with the following benefits:

+ An understanding of how existing and potential customers view and interact with the competition.

+ A sense of your competitor's strengths and weaknesses.

+ A mechanism to develop effective competitive strategies in your target market.

With the rise of the internet and social media, there's a lot of information available that had previously been difficult or costly to gather, including customer perspectives. There's no special trick or secret to completing a competitor analysis. It's just a matter of doing the research and connecting the dots. Here's our process for conducting a competitor analysis.

To start your analysis, you need to identify your competitors. It might seem obvious, but we can't tell you the number of clients who have started building their product without ever realizing that someone else was already doing what they were proposing. Start with a Google search to research who's doing what you want to do.

If you are convinced that no one is doing what you do, consider how people currently solve the problem your product solves. What markets are you potentially disrupting? Pull competitors for your analysis from those markets.

If you are entering market with lots of competition, it's important to figure out which competitors are most important for you to focus on. In a saturated market, you can't (and shouldn't) analyze every competitor. So how do you choose?

To start, focus on companies whose offerings are most similar to yours – companies that offer the same or very similar services and features and have similar product and service differentiators. Also consider companies that have a larger share of the market, particularly big brands. This combination of competitors will give you a good balance of helpful information: You'll glean all you can concerning products and services most closely related to yours by comparing "apples to apples." You'll also know about what the best-known competitors are doing, so you can understand your audiences' base expectations, as well as what is working.

PRO TIP

Focus on 10 or fewer competitors at a time. Depending on your time constraints, you may want to limit it to as few as three. Too many competitors will result in lots of time spent for duplicate information – your competitors will have overlap with each other and your time isn't infinite. Focusing on too few competitors will set you up to miss some valuable information. You'll also miss industry patterns that are critical to understand. As with all research, the idea here is to get information that will help you adjust your business and product toward success. Even if you only have time for one or two, it will help you better understand the market and your customers' expectations. Just build your knowledge over time.

Once you've identified your competitors, you can start your research. The first step in doing this is to identify your overall goal for the data or, more plainly, what questions you are trying to answer. As with all research, defining what you want to get from the effort allows you to focus on the relevant information; otherwise, the amount of data available can be overwhelming. For competitor analyses, there are a few main questions you are likely trying to answer. These include:

+ **How do customers view the companies you identified? What do they like and dislike? In what ways are they frustrated with these companies?** These questions pertain to the company's brand and how the customer feels when interacting with that brand. You may be able to improve customer feelings and use this as a differentiator for your company.

   Brand is easy to overlook in this process, but it's one of the easiest ways to differentiate your product from a competitor. Consider McDonald's vs. Burger King, Walmart vs. Target, or Home Depot vs. Lowe's. You have opinions about which is "best," but fundamentally, these companies offer nearly the same products and services.

+ **What features are the companies offering? How are they executed? What works well? What doesn't work well?** These questions pertain to the company's products and/or services themselves. You may be able to craft a product or service that's "better" than what the competition offers.

Once you've identified the questions you want to focus on, you can get started with the research phase. The research aspect is very straightforward, but it does take some time to complete. Let's walk through the process.

1. **Google [competitor 1].** Open their main site (if they have one), as well as any top articles that come up on the first page of your search results that are relevant to your goal.

2. **Conduct a *5-second test* of the homepage.** View the page for 5 seconds and then toggle to a neutral tab or move away from the computer. Write down what you remember about the site. Based on what you saw, what did you think the site was about? This will give you a sense of their messaging and how they're positioning themselves in the market.

3. **Go back to the competitor's website and review it in more depth.** How is their navigation organized? What features, products, and messages are prioritized? What style of language are they using? How would you describe the style? Which content, interactions, images or aspect of the site stand out as particularly unique or effective? Does anything seem off, odd, or strange?

4. **Identify their main audiences.** Based on what you read and saw on their website, who are they talking to?

5. **Review any lists of product features or service offerings in detail.** How do these differ from what you offer? How are they the same?

6. **Take particular note of their pricing structure.** Do they offer any freemiums, the free-forever versions of their products? What pricing tiers do the offer, if any? Have they called out any offers as "most popular," "best value," or by some other attribute? What differentiates each tier?

7. **View any company or CEO-level social media profiles.** Do they have a Facebook page? An Instagram account? Twitter? YouTube? Linkedin? Review each to understand how they communicate with their customers. Are they very responsive? Do they ignore certain messages or certain people? How are customers responding to them? What are the main reasons that cause customers to contact them on social media?

8. **Look up the competitor on review websites.** Look on Yelp, Better Business Bureau (BBB), Consumer Reports, Angie's List, Google reviews, iTunes reviews, Google Play store reviews, and any other places you find reviews. What do the most favorable reviews say? What do the least favorable reviews say? Is the company responding? How are they responding to their reviews?

9. **Search specifically for customer service-related posts from customers.** Check out any message boards, community forums, help areas, and similar areas; people will go there to post about problems, challenges, frustrations, and needs. This will give you a wealth of information about where your competitors are falling down on the job.

10. **Review the additional tabs you opened during your initial search in step #1.** Is there a lot of buzz around the company? Does anything stand out as particularly good or bad?

11. **Sign up for their free trial.** Pay attention to how their product compares to yours. Are they doing things that you haven't considered? Is some of the UI clunky? Does it *feel* easy? (Whether it's actually easy is irrelevant; feelings matter more.) If you're feeling adventurous, skip to Chapter 9 and conduct usability tests on the free trial to see how customers use it.

PRO TIP

Gather First, then Analyze.

Focus first on information gathering. While it's tempting to draw conclusions as you get information, it's important for a few reasons not to analyze as you go along. First, it's easy to get distracted by the next "shiny thing" that seems conclusive; taking a step back from the information lets you make smart decisions that make sense for your actual business. Additionally, if you analyze as you collect data, you lose the opportunity to aggregate your research and look for overarching patterns. Your impact on the market will be much more successful if you wait and analyze at the end.

This is not meant to be an exhaustive list of research actions for a competitor analysis, but rather a guide to get you started. Once you set your goal, you may find that you need to search for specific information not mentioned here, or that some of the basic suggestions are not helpful. This is normal. At the end of the day, use this as a framework for your thinking and collect the information that's most helpful to your situation.

3. Compare, Contrast, and Analyze the Data

Once you've successfully collected all the information you need (or could find), it's time to pull it all together. There are lots of ways to analyze data; it all comes back to interpreting the data collected and finding patterns that affect your business. The first thing to do is to aggregate all your data by question. For example, if you did a 5-second test for each competitor, list your impressions of each, and note any overlaps between the websites. Do this for each piece of information you collected. Tally up overlaps; if you identified both Competitor A and Competitor D as "overly verbose" in your 5-second test, that piece gets two tally marks.

PRO TIP

Correlation is not Causation

It's definitely possible to have correlation without causation, so be cautious when coming to conclusions. The best way to avoid this is through usability testing (learn how in Chapter 9), which provides insight into the "why" of what's happening. Maybe customers were confused by a weird typo in the product rather than the content itself. Whenever possible, validate your conclusions.

PRO TIP

Check Yourself

Once you're established, you can also do a competitor analysis on yourself so you can understand where you fit in the mix. This will also help you see any gaps or potential problem areas in with your own company.

Next, aggregate further and look for patterns and connections between the different questions you asked. For example, if your 5-second test revealed that most sites are "overly verbose," and those same companies have customer feedback that things are "confusing," you've found a pattern. Pay attentions to patterns that are the most relevant to your research goal and your business goals. If you have some competitors whose data you care about more, you can weight your analysis, giving them two tally marks per other competitors' one mark.

Once you create a list of identified patterns, go back to your business and project plans: How should you adjust your product, marketing, or company position? Are you offering something whose benefit will outweigh the cost of switching to and learning a new product? If not, where can you add, remove, or change something to overcome that barrier? Should you restructure your pricing? To do this well and determine next steps, you may also want to research some marketing psychology basics so you can better understand what is and isn't effective for reaching people.

And that's it: a basic but effective competitor analysis process. Unlike direct customer research, you don't often need to repeat this effort in full. You can repeat it on a smaller scale to expand your offerings or vet new key players who are joining the market. The baseline you generate today will give you a great start for your continued analysis for a long time.

Summary

Research is a critical step in planning your product. It helps you validate your assumptions, generate product ideas, and make informed design decisions. We recommend two main methods of research: customer interviews and competitor analyses.

Conducting well-planned customer interviews gives you real-world insight into your target audience's goals, needs, and challenges. To get the most out of each interview, prepare a comprehensive interview plan and word your questions carefully. Competitor analysis helps you position yourself strategically in the market, and reveals gaps that your product could fill. It also helps you understand your audiences' expectations and mental models from existing solutions. Your product is only as good as the research it's based on. Don't skip it.

Put It in Action

Research has two main components: Market/competition and your customers. You'll need a good understanding of both to succeed. In the workbook, identify any competitors (or reference your list from your Business Canvas worksheets) and fill in the competitor spreadsheet for each one you research. Then complete the analysis worksheet to bring everything together, summarizing your findings about the market and industry.

For your customers, identify your target audience and consider how you can reach people. Note the methods you will try in your customer interviews planning sheet. Document assumptions, open questions and overall what you need to know about your primary audience. From there brainstorm and finalize your research questions in the workbook and schedule your customer interviews. Use the customer findings spreadsheet to collect information and look for patterns. Finalize your knowledge (including any outstanding questions or assumptions). We'll use this research to create a persona, in Chapter 4.

IDEA VALIDATION **DESIGN**

Define Your Audience

CHAPTER FOUR

Personas are archetypes of users that are based on research from actual users.

Also referred to as a *target audience* or *ideal client*, a *persona* becomes a representation of a group of users with the same (or closely related) goals, needs, behaviors, and contexts. Personas help focus a project and your product, allowing you to make clearer decisions about what features and workflows to include in your product, and how it should be designed and organized.

Additionally, personas give everyone on the team a point of reference for every action. At any point, someone might ask, "Why are we doing this?" Personas can help you point to a real answer – or lead to a decision to nix the activity or project if you don't have an answer. As we saw in the "three goals" story about Jen's real estate client in Chapter 1, personas give clarity about the users' goals and they help your team and stakeholders break out of their own perspectives. This clarity is especially helpful because people generally make decisions based on asking, "Does this make sense to me?" With personas, ask instead, "Does this make sense to our users?" and have more success in answering that question accurately. Ultimately, personas help you make product and design decisions that are tailored to your target audience instead of yourself.

Creating Personas

To create personas, you look for patterns of behavior that are common among a subset of your user-base and create a fictitious person to represent each set of patterns. Personas are best created from research; for example, you might use the customer interview method outlined in Chapter 3. While this may seem like an obvious statement, most personas start out as proto-personas: personas created from an internal team's educated assumptions about who their audience is, rather by researching first. In this chapter we will cover how to do both.

Research-Based Personas

Research-based personas are created from research and conversations with actual customers, which we cover in Chapter 3: Conduct Your Research. The data points from each session are collected and reviewed for patterns. Each pattern becomes a different persona, identifying a different audience for your product.

To create research-based personas, you'll need some research findings to work from; these findings are most often gathered through customer interviews and ethnographic studies (see Chapter 3). You can also work from surveys and market research, although the best information comes from direct conversations and observation. The steps for creating a persona from research are as follows:

1. Identify the variables for each persona.

2. Map each study participant to the variables.

3. Look for variable patterns of two or more participants.

4. Write up each pattern identified in step three as a persona.

5. Repeat steps 3 and 4 for each additional pattern.

The following sections look at the 5 main steps in more depth.

PRO TIP

Keep Personas Dynamic.

It can be tempting to create your personas once, set it and forget it style. However, personas can get outdated quickly, so it's best to revisit them for accuracy and relevance regularly, usually at least once every 6 months. It's also good to check in with your teams when you do this, to help keep alignment and make sure everyone still has your personas top of mind.

Variables are the behaviors and demographics of people in your target audience. Use the research questions you asked during your customer interviews to create variables for your personas. For example, if you asked about someone's habits in checking email throughout their day, "email checking habits" would become a variable. Here's a list of common categories that variables fall into that may help you get started in defining your specific variables:

+ **Skills** – areas of expertise or competence

+ **Pain points** – areas of struggle or aggravation

+ **Goals** – the end result the a person wants to complete

+ **Mental models** – conscious and unconscious expectations about how something should be or work (see Chapter 7 for more details)

+ **Frustrations** – annoyances, failures, and dissatisfaction

+ **Priorities** – things or ideas the interviewee cares about the most

+ **Relationships** – interactions with other people

+ **Context** – where, when, and how the interviewee accesses the product

+ **Attitudes** – feelings, emotions, and perspectives

+ **Behaviors** – habits, methods, actions, and activities

This is not an exhaustive list, and not all of these categories will be relevant for every product. Once you've identified your variable list, determine the range of responses for each variable. Most variables can be represented by a spectrum from one extreme to another. Some variables will have more discrete choices, one of which will apply to each interviewee. If you're not certain what the spectrum should be for each variable, look at the responses you received to the question or the observations you made about that variable; the range of responses will give you a starting point. For each variable, you only need to consider the range of possibilities that fall within the answers you have collected.

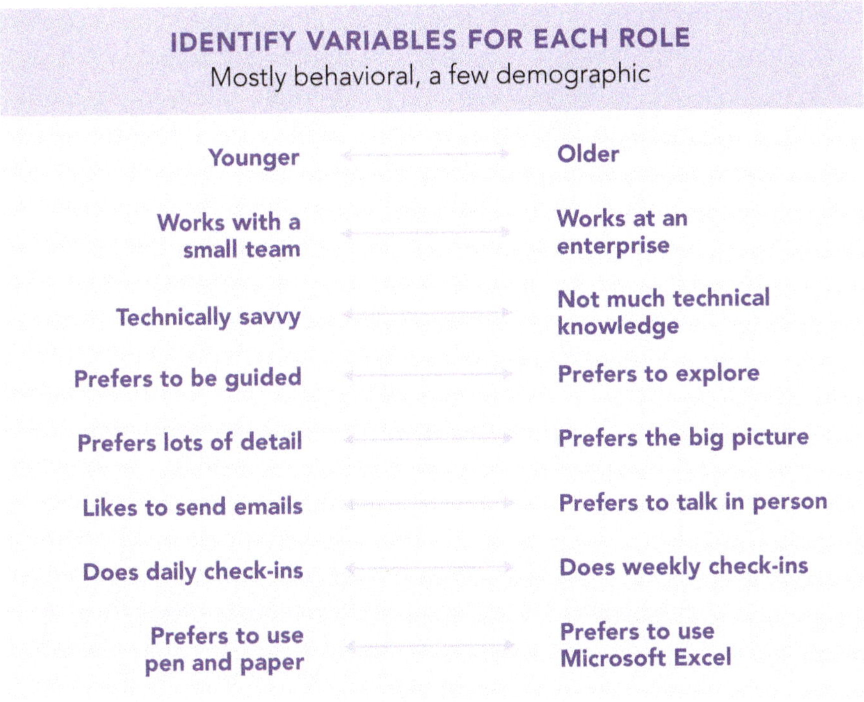

IDENTIFY VARIABLES FOR EACH ROLE
Mostly behavioral, a few demographic

Younger	**Older**
Works with a small team	**Works at an enterprise**
Technically savvy	**Not much technical knowledge**
Prefers to be guided	**Prefers to explore**
Prefers lots of detail	**Prefers the big picture**
Likes to send emails	**Prefers to talk in person**
Does daily check-ins	**Does weekly check-ins**
Prefers to use pen and paper	**Prefers to use Microsoft Excel**

Figure 4.1: Identifying spectra for evaluating personas.

Most of your variables should revolve around behavior, frustrations, goals, or context, rather than demographics. Not all members of a certain demographic exhibit a certain behavior, experience the same frustrations, or have a shared context or goal.

2. Map Each Study Participant to the Variables

Once you've created a list of variables and identified the spectrum for each variable, you can start mapping each participant to the variables. Each participant should occupy a maximum of one spot for each variable, even if they gave answers to support multiple spots on your spectrum. In that case, choose the most likely or most common spot for that participant, or create a spectrum that supports varied behavior. For example, if your variable is "method for checking email" you can create one spot on the spectrum to be "uses phone sometimes and laptop sometimes".

It's also the case that you may not have information about all participants for all variables. If you don't observe a participant exhibiting a certain behavior, do not guess at what they would do or where they fall on the spectrum. Simply leave them off for that variable.

The example in Figure 4.2 shows what it might look like to map interviewees to two different variables.

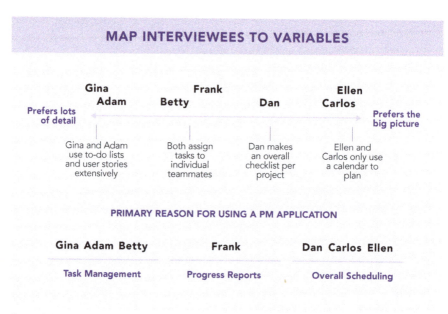

Figure 4.2: A continuous variable versus a discrete choice variable.

This example demonstrates a spectrum variable, and a variable with discrete choices. For the spectrum variable, explanatory notes are included to identify what that area of the spectrum means for those participants. This is particularly important, as otherwise those "in-between" slots would be meaningless or open to a variety of interpretations. Above all, you want to be precise in the information you've collected and in how it maps to your participants.

Once you've finished mapping all your participants, it's time to start looking for patterns. These patterns will become the basis for your personas. The important thing to note when looking for patterns is that you want patterns that persist for the same set of participants across multiple variables. What does that mean? Look again at Figure 4.2. Notice that Betty and Frank are similar in the first behavior about plan detail preferences. However, they are not the same in the second behavior, primary reason for using a PM tool. Therefore, if you created a persona from the Betty/Frank combination, you would not include that information. Figure 4.3 illustrates this logic in a more complete context.

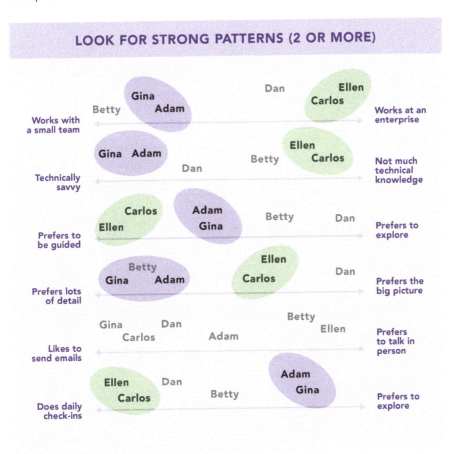

LOOK FOR STRONG PATTERNS (2 OR MORE)

Figure 4.3: Look for patterns where two or more people have the same or similar habits within your variable spectra.

As you can see in Figure 4.3, when we look at multiple variables, some patterns start to emerge. Now we have the foundation for two personas, as outlined in Figure 4.4. (Note: You will probably have many more variables than this to consider, resulting in more personas to consider.)

EACH PATTERN IS THE BASIS FOR A PERSONA

PATTERN #1

+ Works with a fairly small team
+ Technically savvy
+ Prefers a mix between guided & exploratory
+ Tends to prefer more detail
+ Does weekly check-ins

PATTERN #2

+ Works at an enterprise
+ Not so technically savvy
+ Prefers to be guided
+ Prefers the bigger picture
+ Does daily check-ins

Figure 4.4: Consistent groupings become behavior patterns for a future persona.

Once you've identified your persona patterns, it's time to put it together into a useful format: the persona.

It's important to consider what persona format is most helpful for your team; the creation and use of personas can vary widely. Many of the teams I've worked with have had success with the format we will use below. This includes:

+ **A name:** Give your persona a real name. Don't call them "Tester #1" or "Joe Schmo." Part of the goal of personas is to have your team connect with the persona, keeping them in mind as they complete the project. Demographics may be important depending on the patterns you've identified in your research, so make sure the name matches the demographic. Be careful not to reinforce racial or gender stereotypes though.

+ **A quote**: If this persona could communicate one thing they want to accomplish, or a frustration they want to vent, what would it be? You may draw on something particularly relevant that an interviewee told you.

+ **Goals**: What are the target audience goals for this persona?

+ **Frustrations**: What is frustrating to this persona now? Perhaps there's no workflow that works for them, or they can't find something on the website that should be there, or they don't understand some concept the website should convey more clearly.

+ **Tasks**: What kinds of tasks must this persona accomplish? These do not need to be in great detail. For example: purchase a shirt on the website, check the status of something, pay a bill, etc.

PRO TIP

Do you need a photo?

It's common to include a photo in your persona. The reason being a deeper personal connection and better remembrance of the personas. However, when you include a photo, you also open yourself up to the biases that photo emphasizes. Age, race, and gender are fundamental demographics that are set by an image, whether intended or not. It's up to you whether the use of a photo furthers your success in using personas. However, if you're in an industry open to biases like racism or sexism, opt to leave the photo out. And above all, treat your personas as the diverse demographics they represent, so you can successfully serve your full audience.

As you can see in Figure 4.5, our persona, Paul Hayden, encapsulates the details we identified for "pattern 2" in Figure 7, while expanding them to create a complete profile. So how do you get there from here?

Research-based Persona
PAUL HAYDEN

NARRATIVE

Paul works as a Product Manager for GloboTech's database management software app. He needs to keep on top of the current release cycle and the activities of his team of 4 designers and 14 developers. Every day, he logs into the company's PM tool to view alerts and review the upcoming calendar. When a milestone is approaching, he needs to check- in often with the team members involved in the delivery.

GOALS

+ Get release done on schedule

+ Support his team when they run into problems

+ Be able to tell his supervisors how the project is going during the weekly management team meetings

" I just want to see what's relevant to this week; I don't need to spend tons of time filling out a lot of detail for every little thing."

FRUSTRATIONS

+ Having to learn new software is an annoyance

+ It's often hard to find the lower-level features and details that his team members sometimes use inside the PM tool.

TASKS

+ Review the project status everyday

+ Schedule deliver check-in meetings with relevant tea members

+ Download weekly reports on his team's resource usage

Figure 4.5: Final Persona, Paul Hayden.

Once you've identified a pattern, start by looking at which goals are a part of the pattern. These goals give you a window into that pattern's motivations. By understanding a persona's motivations, you can easily add detail to the other elements of that pattern. Focus on updating any vagaries and making decisions about missing information. It's especially important to consider the reported challenges and frustrations that are contained in this pattern; calling those out explicitly will make your persona more useful. Sometimes, these frustrations are not obviously stated. In those instances, come back to the goals and the experiences of the persona: Where do they disconnect? Those are areas of frustration.

5. Finalize Your Persona

Once you've narrowed down your personas, it's time to add the final details. A contextual story or narrative helps people make a deeper, more empathetic connection to the persona; it also breaks up the persona details, which are mostly in list format. When writing the story, consider what the key goals and frustrations of the persona are. How do they fit into the context of the persona's work? This will help you write a clear, helpful story.

Next, create a summary quote (in purple, under the photo, in Figure 4.5). The quote provides a quick sound bite that summarizes the persona's perspective. Writing a good summary quote can be a challenge; because you're trying to capture the essence of the persona in a quick sentence, it may take a few iterations to really nail it. If you get stuck, you can even use a quote from an actual customer interview, if it fits the persona. Put these pieces together with the goals, tasks, and frustrations and you have your final persona.

PRO TIP

Combine for Best Results

As you finalize your personas, you may find that it makes sense to combine some. Because personas are helpful only insofar as they represent differences that will result in different experiences, some personas may be extraneous or redundant. Combine and refine your personas until you feel they are purposeful, relevantly different, and clear.

Proto-Personas

As mentioned at the beginning of this chapter, *proto-personas* are created from internal group consensus about who the audience is. While they are completely assumption-based and have a high potential to be inaccurate, they can be helpful because they give the team a shared understanding and focus for moving forward. Proto-personas are not ideal, but they're better than not creating any personas (or shared understanding of audiences).

When creating proto-personas, it's important to capture information that's similar to what you would collect through customer interviews and ethnographic studies. One way to do this is to interview the members of your team as you would your customers, only instead of talking about their own experiences, your team members would answer for the customer. Then you can follow a process similar to the one used when creating research-based personas; however, you'll want to use more discretionary judgment in making final persona decisions, as the data is all assumption-based.

Another method for creating proto-personas is to use empathy mapping.

Empathy mapping is a technique developed by Dave Gray, in which you ask meeting attendees (usually your team members and stakeholders) to empathize with and understand a specific audience by considering what they think, feel, see, say, do, and hear, as well as the pains they face and the benefits you can offer them.

Conducting an Empathy Mapping Workshop

When creating empathy maps, schedule a meeting with as many stakeholders and executives as you can get to attend. Once your meeting is scheduled, send an update describing the target audiences you will be discussing in each session, so meeting attendees can come prepared to discuss those audiences. This will give you the best, most thorough information. Sending the pre-meeting update will also help circumvent "changes of heart" wherein someone decides they have different "information" about the audience after the meeting is over, as they'll have had time to process through their thoughts before the meeting instead of after.

Empathy mapping is a straightforward activity on the surface, but actually getting your team to drop their assumptions and put themselves in your audience's shoes might require additional finessing. Prepare in advance by drawing an empathy map canvas (or figure) on a large poster, flipchart, or whiteboard for each audience, like the one shown in Figure 4.6. Alternatively, you can project an image of the map onto a wall and only use sticky notes (just don't accidentally write on the wall!).

PRO TIP

Be sure to get as many perspectives as possible in the room when running the empathy mapping workshop, especially those of your stakeholders and executives. Reschedule if you have to! Having stakeholders in your meetings is essential for determining the right target audiences to create into personas.

Empathy Map Canvas

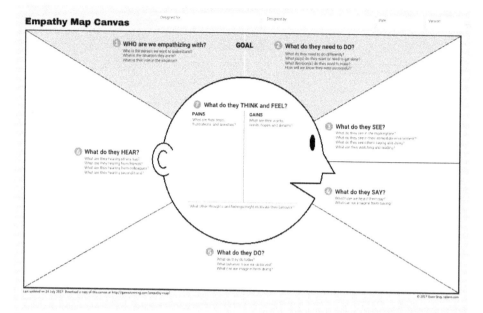

Figure 4.6: Empathy map template, demonstrating what a given persona does, sees, says, and hears, as well as what they think and feel. By Dave Gray.
http://gamestorming.com/wp-content/uploads/2017/07/Empathy-Map-Canvas-006.pdf

Once your empathy map canvases are all set up, define your focus question. For the most part, your focus question will be something along the lines of "What is life like for [audience] when they use [our product]?" Another one would be "How is life for [audience] when they try to [solve the problem our product solves] without [our product]?" Essentially, you want to hone in on the times and context around when someone would be using your product, the reasons they might need your product, and what their life is like now without it. The focus question should be how you lead off your meeting.

After you establish the focus question, remind everyone that they need to consider the answer to this question from the perspective of the audience you are working on, rather than their own. Then walk through each of the sections one by one to fill in experiences for the audience. If you have a more experienced team you can ask them to generate ideas for all of the sections as they think of them.

As the moderator, you can decide how to handle each idea: Either write it directly on your canvas or, as mentioned before, use one sticky note per idea. Each section is meant to focus on a sensory experience: what an audience is thinking, feeling, seeing, saying, doing, and hearing. Take additional time in the thinking and feeling section. Consider the pain or frustrations of each audience; these are the problems you want to be solving. In the "gains" section, list the benefits that your product provides: How are you making this audience's lives better?

Be sure to walk through the final "results" for each empathy map before moving on to the next one, so everyone can confirm that they are on board with the final map and, by extension, the final proto-persona. It's also a good idea to take photos of your finalized empathy maps; this makes it easier to keep track ofthe information without having to manage a large empathy map or piles of sticky notes after the meeting is done.

Once you have your completed empathy maps, you'll need to turn them into proto-personas. The good news is that this process is the same as for research-based personas. Essentially, an empathy map provides the "pattern" for a persona. From here, follow the instructions in steps four (write up the pattern as a persona) and five (finalize your persona). Once you've done this, it's important to get feedback on the final persona from the team you worked with. Because these personas are created from that team's input directly, you may get some pushback on decisions you made about what to include and what not to include, especially if people have strong opinions about who the personas are. Be prepared to rationalize your decisions and, as soon as possible, do research to validate or update the assumptions in your proto-personas.

Summary

Gathering data and doing research on your audience isn't enough. You need to put that data into a useful, helpful format: personas. Well-designed personas give your project focus, and enable you to make informed design decisions. Developing relevant, accurate personas can be time-consuming, but the effort is worthwhile.

To create personas, use the research from your customer interviews and competitor analyses to identify different audiences. Validate your conclusions and assumptions, and refine your personas over time as you learn more about your target audience.

If research-based personas are out of scope for your project, proto-personas and empathy mapping can provide an acceptable starting point that will align your team and keep you focused. When using proto-personas, validate your assumptions as more research-based information becomes available.

Above all, refer to your personas frequently during implementation. Ensure that every project-related action supports your personas' goals, needs, contexts, and mental models.

Put It in Action

Your customers (or potential customers) are the lifeblood of your product's success, so it's important to keep them top of mind. Using your research from Chapter 3, create one or more personas for your product, using the persona worksheets and the process outlined in this chapter.

If you weren't able to do customer interviews or you want to start by getting team alignment and capturing assumptions, conduct an empathy mapping exercise with your team, using the template found at *www.gamestorming. com/wp-content/uploads/2017/07/Empathy-Map-Canvas-006.pdf*. Complete the empathy mapping exercise for each persona and then use your workbook to finalize each proto-persona, including listing out assumptions and open questions. Be sure to validate any proto-personas with research as soon as possible.

Use your persona (or proto-persona) to help guide your decisions throughout the rest of your activities, especially when there's a difference of opinion or moment of uncertainty.

DESIGN

IDEA

PLANNING

Establish Your Brand

CHAPTER FIVE

When you think of the Transportation Security Administration (TSA), what comes to mind?

You might say:

+ Airport security

+ Long lines

+ Plastic tubs

+ Conveyor belts

+ Removing shoes

+ Pat-downs

+ Body-scan machines

+ People with uniforms

If I asked you to think of three words that describe the TSA, you might say unfriendly, disruptive, and invasive. As you deal with the TSA, you might feel bored and frustrated by the chaos, or amused and entertained by people who can't follow directions, or grateful that screening is happening to keep everyone safe.

Now if I asked you about the TSA brand, you might draw a blank. After all, you might not know what their logo looks like exactly, or if they have a tagline or slogan. You may not know exactly what their colors are, although you might remember blue uniforms at the airport.

Figure 5.1: Screenshot of the TSA logo.

Does the logo shown in Figure 5.1 help build your trust and make you feel safe while flying? What if the logo was red or if it had a slogan? Would that help or hurt? For the TSA, having a red logo might feel more on-brand, but only because of the existing negative connotations of the brand, coupled with red's feelings of fire, rage and anger.

Of course, brand isn't limited to logos, slogans, and colors. The TSA brand has almost nothing to do with their logo. Instead, it's best to think of a brand as a series of attributes that form the perception and personality of an organization. The experience you have while interacting with the entity is a critical piece of how you perceive that brand. What experience can you expect from a brand? Is that experience consistent across both physical and virtual locations? Does the brand's voice on social media match the rest of the brand? What is the organization not saying that's part of the brand?

Most people want to start and end with colors, logos, and slogans. However, this is the easiest and least impactful part of creating your brand. Your products, including websites, applications, social media accounts, and physical locations, need to represent more than just the colors, logos, and slogans of your organization. They need to evoke intentional feelings and experiences. But how do you create these intangible assets of your brand?

Every element you add to your website, every required field on your form, every widget and gadget and sentence you write, contribute to your brand. For example, designating a form field as required sends the message that the organization can't complete the interaction without this piece of information. Is that true? If so, require it. An email address on a contact form is a good example of a required field: How can you answer the visitor's question without a way to reach them? But do you also need their mailing address, birthday, gender, and favorite color? When you ask these questions, are you building your customer database, or are you building trust in your brand? If you're really trying to build trust in your brand, don't require that information.

Brand is also built through interaction, much more definitively than through any logos or slogans. Recently, United Airlines saw just how true this could be. Over 50 years, United created and seemed to embody the "Fly the Friendly Skies" slogan. However, in April 2017, any belief in that sentiment flew right out the window for most United customers. The company of "friendly skies" did one of the most unfriendly things imaginable: They physically dragged a passenger out of his seat and off the plane to make room for a United employee, causing several injuries to the passenger in the process.

Onlooking passengers captured the whole event on their smartphones and the social media video posts went viral almost immediately. The resulting weeks brought United under intense public scrutiny, as countless individuals, media outlets, and celebrities pointed out the hypocrisy and inconsistency in United's brand.

Ava DuVernay ✓
@ava

This could be me or you next time. Shame on @United who broke customer trust + instigated this. Shame on the airport cops. Cowardly assault.

 Jayse D. Anspach @JayseDavid
@United overbook #flight3411 and decided to force random passengers off the plane. Here's how they did it:

0:51

10:11 AM - 10 Apr 2017

1,819 Retweets **3,513** Likes

Figure 5.2: A response to the viral video of a United passenger dragged from an airplane.

More positively, the Wendy's Twitter account continues to make waves with its sassy, sometimes irreverent tone, all in favor of promoting Wendy's fast food as superior to all others. Wendy's knew they had an opportunity to connect with younger generations, and they nailed it. Most significant was the #NuggsForCarter trend. Carter Wilkerson inquired of the social media account, "How many retweets for a year of free chicken nuggets?" Giving Wilkerson a goal of 18 million retweets, the Wendy's Twitter account set in motion the trend that resulted in the most retweeted tweet of all time (as of the writing of this book) – Wilkerson's tweet request for free chicken nuggets.

Figure 5.3: Wendy's highlighting their success in the #NuggsForCarter campaign.

The follow-up was also on point. One Twitter user asked Wendy's, "How many people asked for a rt [retweet] deal after this got popular," to which Wendy's coolly replied, "18 million," bringing it all home again. Wendy's has remained competitive and established a clear 21st century brand that goes beyond logo and color.

Figure 5.4: Wendy's demonstrates their brand in a typical social media interaction.

While you might easily recognize logos for United and Wendy's, you're likely to also have an emotional reaction, whether positive or negative, to these brands! This emotional reaction is a critical aspect of branding that isn't discussed nearly as often as logos and colors. To get that emotional reaction, first consider the tone and voice of your brand.

Voice and Tone

Voice and tone refers to the writing and communication style of your brand. Consider your expectations when communicating with various types of organizations:

+ **A bank:** Trustworthy, responsible, confident
+ **A university:** Educated, informed, inviting
+ **Online shopping:** Efficient, fun, engaging

Despite the lack of specifics, you probably thought immediately of companies in each category that both did and did not match the listed attributes. Now run this same exercise with your own industry and brand. Did you come up with attributes that make sense in your industry? How do those industry attributes match your brand's current attributes? This will give you a starting point for creating your company's voice and tone.

You can apply the updated voice and tone when you revise existing materials for your organization, including the current website, apps, social media, press releases, brochures, TV and radio advertisements, or any other communications media used by your organization. You can also create new content and manage social media and help-desk accounts. Full details for creating a tone and voice table (the structure for defining your tone and voice) can be found in Chapter 6.

It's critical to be consistent in your brand, staying true to the impression you want to create. Therefore, one of the keys to success for your website or app is making sure that it reinforces your brand.

Branding Information

If you work for an established organization, chances are that the visual brand elements were established long ago. In this case, you can check with the marketing department for a *brand style guide*. This type of guide typically contains a list of approved colors with usage context; logo variations of different sizes, shapes, and colors, including usage style restrictions; approved fonts; and other design elements. If you're lucky, your organization's brand style guide is in an easily digestible format. Occasionally, you'll find that these standards are established, but they've never been compiled into an official document.

You may also have a content style guide, which covers how language is used, what terminology is used at what time, examples of how to write, a voice and tone table and more. This will be discussed in Chapter 6, Content.

A thorough brand style guide includes usage information about colors, as shown in Figure 5.5:

Standard UI Colors

	#EEEEEE	Light gray	Main background color
	#333333	Dark gray	Default text color
	#f5554b	Salmon	Primary accent color
	#48cdbf	Teal	Secondary accent color
	#272E32	Black	Header bar color
	#FFFFFF	White	Content panel color

Figure 5.5: Basic brand colors, including how these colors are used on the website.

Some color usage instructions may include detailed information that's specific to product or brand requirements. In the example shown in Figure 5.6, the colors may not be part of the brand, but they are important for creating a well-designed user interface. Note that the specific colors in the figure refer to certain types of interactions.

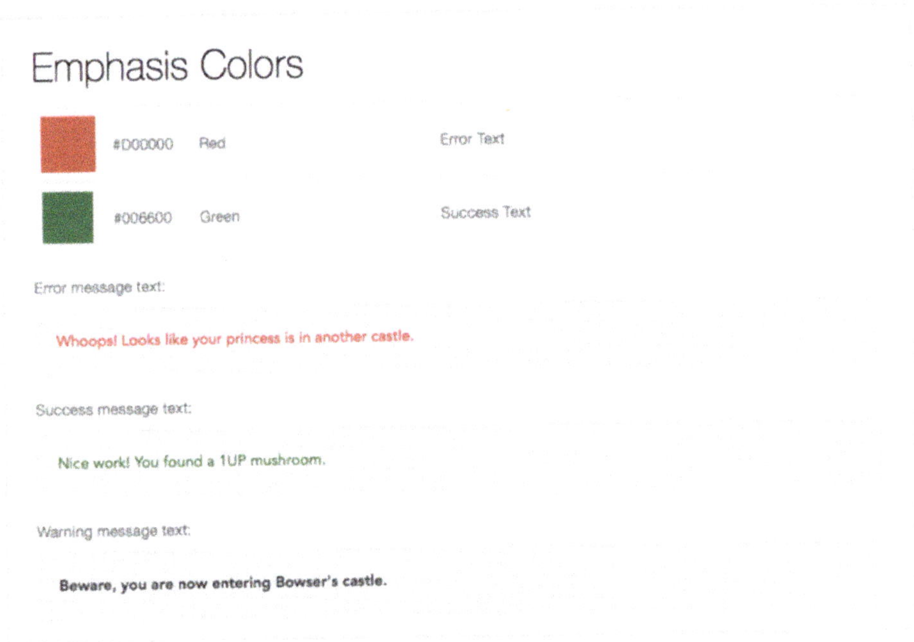

Emphasis Colors

■	#D00000	Red	Error Text
■	#006600	Green	Success Text

Error message text:

Whoops! Looks like your princess is in another castle.

Success message text:

Nice work! You found a 1UP mushroom.

Warning message text:

Beware, you are now entering Bowser's castle.

Figure 5.6: Colors important to the interface but not the brand.

Information about approved fonts, including sizes and weights, is also useful. Sometimes web fonts will differ from fonts used in press releases, due to either legibility concerns or online availability. Figure 5.7 demonstrates how an approved font guide would provide helpful brand information including examples, sizes, and any specified fallback fonts.

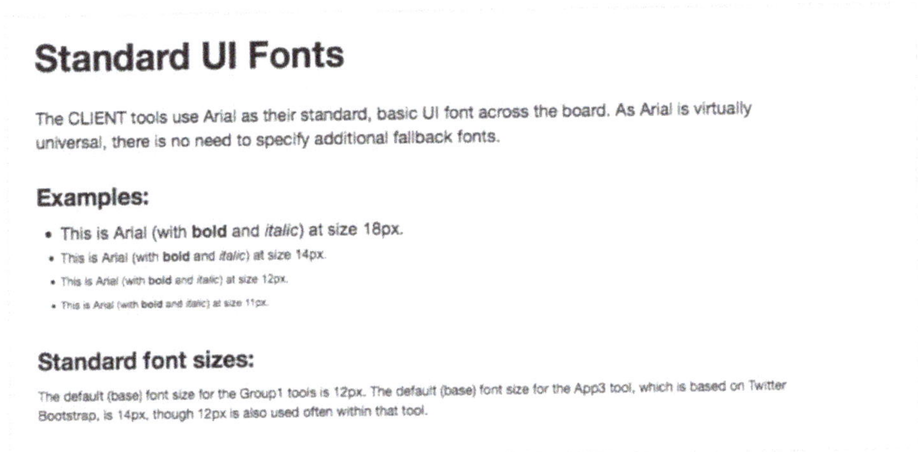

Standard UI Fonts

The CLIENT tools use Arial as their standard, basic UI font across the board. As Arial is virtually universal, there is no need to specify additional fallback fonts.

Examples:

- This is Arial (with **bold** and *italic*) at size 18px.
- This is Arial (with **bold** and *italic*) at size 14px.
- This is Arial (with **bold** and *italic*) at size 12px.
- This is Arial (with **bold** and *italic*) at size 11px.

Standard font sizes:

The default (base) font size for the Group1 tools is 12px. The default (base) font size for the App3 tool, which is based on Twitter Bootstrap, is 14px, though 12px is also used often within that tool.

Figure 5.7: A sample methodology for specifying standard user interface (UI) fonts.

Finally, almost all brands have multiple versions of the logo for various uses. For example, a brand style guide might include the main logo in full color, a reversed logo for dark backgrounds, a square or circular version, and a small version specifically designed for use as a favicon, as seen in figure 5.8. Your brand may also include additional color variations, like a black and white version that's optimized for print materials.

Figure 5.8: Examples of different logo treatments for different uses.

If you are creating a new organization, or if your brand has not been established adequately in an existing organization, now is a great time to create a simple logo. While it may seem like a good idea to spend weeks creating and iterating on a complicated logo, you'll get just as much value keeping it simple. Just look to Google, Apple, and other big names to see this in action. Create a logo that's text-based in a font that speaks to your brand's attributes with the intention of revisiting it later as your brand evolves. You'll save time and money by doing this.

Interaction Elements

Every project team and stakeholder we've ever worked with has told us, "I want to make it simple and intuitive to use." No one ever requests a product that's complex and complicated. When everyone wants "simple and intuitive," how do we interpret and achieve that in a meaningful way?

We suggest *interaction elements*; these are any elements in your interface that do something. This category spans the full breadth of interaction on the web and computers in general – from a basic link to another page, to a form that captures data, to a search query results page, to a full-featured game.

It's easy (and often expected) to include these elements in your product. For a simple start, look to frameworks like Bootstrap, Foundation, or UIkit. All of these frameworks contain dozens of JavaScript-based widgets that are easily dropped into a product for all types of interactivity. In content management systems like Joomla, WordPress, and Drupal, there are thousands of options for elements that add various types of interactivity. However, before you create the interactive site of your imagination, ask yourself if the interactivity is congruent with your brand and goals. Just because you can add something doesn't mean you should.

It helps to spell out exactly how you'll evaluate interaction elements to determine whether they're the right fit for your product. Since "simple and intuitive" are not great criteria, we've created some common interaction elements to consider instead. You may also think of these in terms of a pattern library or design system.

Common Patterns vs. Specialized or Need-To-Learn

A common pattern is one that's seen all over the internet. The most basic example of this is a text link. Blue and underlined, it's possibly the most universally recognized interaction element on the web. Simply click and it takes you somewhere else. Could you imagine if someone wrote all their site copy in that same underlined blue text? Talk about confusing! As new link patterns emerge, the styling of a link may be different, but the basic concept of underlined and blue will always signal "link." This common pattern is unlikely to go away, regardless of newer ideas for how to handle links.

Think of other common patterns you see online: image galleries, "read more" buttons and links, a news teaser, or a shopping cart page. Icons are also common and worth copying: save, print, and undo are just some of the icons that are standard across sites, and software in general. These are just some of the countless patterns that you can include on your website without reinventing the wheel.

A specialized interface involves unique patterns and interactions not commonly used in most products, whether it is a unique variation on an existing interface or a new interface that must be designed from scratch. For example, Heather consulted with a client who wanted to display reconstructions of the Egyptian pyramids from the Giza plateau in three dimensions, in an interactive way, on a website. That's an atypical interface, one that might require some learning on the part of the user to maximize their experience.

As you create your product, consider what common patterns you will use and where you will need some form of specialized interface. And when in doubt, start with a common pattern until it's clear the pattern just doesn't work for your product. In most cases, you'll be able to customize a pattern to your product's needs instead of creating something brand new.

Open vs. Proprietary

Open source software is software that's distributed with its source code, making it editable by anyone with an interest in doing so. *Proprietary software* does not allow you to access the source code, meaning you cannot modify the software on an individual level through the code.

When you purchase a piece of software like Microsoft Word, you are only purchasing a license to use the product. Microsoft still owns the source code. If you want to add a new feature to Word, your only course of action is to contact Microsoft and ask for the feature. Unfortunately, there's no guarantee that your feature will be included in the next release or even considered at all. The upside is that most proprietary software like Word has strong support, including a dedicated development team. That often means that the software contains fewer bugs and the existing bugs get fixed more quickly and efficiently.

In contrast, if you download a copy of Open Office, you have the rights to view and modify the source code. You can share the changes you make as well. However, this type of software isn't as well supported, except by volunteer community members; you may find bugs or wish for features for years before seeing any changes, unless you can make them yourself. It's also important to do your research – open source software often has rules or requirements on how you can use it, including whether or not you are able to use it to make money.

With this in mind, consider how you plan to provide access to the interface and code you create for your project. Are you building a product with open source or proprietary tools? Will your product be open source or proprietary? If it's open source, will you distribute the code? What kind of community will you try to build around it? By answering these questions, you'll be able to determine the access level of your product

Scroll vs. Click

Consider how people will move from one section of information to another in the product you're building. In your estimation, would they spend more time clicking or scrolling? Why?

Most products make use of both click and scroll for interactions. However, the best products have considered the need that each interaction is filling and whether those needs are best served by scroll or click.

For example, you could build your product in the style of Facebook, Twitter, or Pinterest, where users can scroll forever, and more information will be loaded as long as the user continues to scroll. Infinite scroll or single-page web applications (SPAs) are two other examples of continuous scrolling. Using parallax scrolling (when the background image scrolls as you scroll on a page) and in-page anchors (when you link to other sections of the same page), the entire product can be presented in a single document and, if you incorporate the infinite scroll, one that never ends.

Alternatively, you could have separate screens of information where accessing different information requires clicking to a new page to get the information. E-commerce sites like Etsy and Amazon, news websites like the Washington Post and the Harvard Business Review, and financial-institution sites like those for Discover Card and Ally Bank are configured in this way.

While there's a certain amount of sizzle to an infinitely scrolling page, consider if infinite scrolling actually serves the goals of either your business or your users. Some interactions may be obviously suited to either scroll or click, and some decisions may come down to research and user preference.

Browse vs. Accomplish

People visit websites for different reasons. On social media, they're likely looking for a connection with their family and friends by viewing posts about what people are doing; there's not a specific task to accomplish. Browsing allows them to accomplish their more nebulous goal of connection. New baby photos? Yes, view now! A video of someone's latest FarmVille update? Scroll past that, please! In browse-oriented products, visitors and users are able to peruse large swaths of information and go where their interests take them (think Wikipedia). It's unlikely that this type of user will have a firm plan for what they'll be doing before they arrive on the site.

Contrast this with a banking website. People aren't visiting banking sites just for fun, even if they enjoy number crunching. They have very specific goals to accomplish: making a deposit, checking an account balance, or transferring money. They want to get this task accomplished as quickly as possible so they can move on to something more fun and interesting like checking their Facebook feed.

When you consider your product, ask yourself which approach supports your personas' goals: browse or accomplish? It may depend on where they are in their own individual goals: Are they browsing some options or focused on specific actions?

One Path vs. Many Options

Most e-commerce websites allow browsing through any order of pages across their website. You don't need to peruse the items in a strictly linear fashion. Instead you can filter, search, and sort through lists of online goods, giving you maximum flexibility to go wherever you want. There are many options for how you can interact with the website with a *browsing mentality*.

However, once you start the checkout process, there is only one path to completing the task. You follow screens of information asking for billing and shipping addresses, coupons, and payment options. There aren't many options, if any, for doing anything else. The retailer wants to get you through the order process without distracting you from completing your purchase! This represents an *accomplish mentality.*

A browsing mentality likely leads to many options for interacting with a site, while an accomplish mentality is often tied to one or a few limited paths. Consider which is most appropriate for your product, or how you'll combine the two in different parts of the website.

User-Led Interactions vs. Site-Guided Interactions

Can users forge their own path on your website? Do they have options for exploring information? If so, you've designed user-led interactions, where the user can choose what happens next. Most websites work like this, with few hints or directions about where to go next.

A site-guided interaction, however, is one in which the product provides directions, instructions, or suggestions for the next steps that a user should take. Some of these websites also follow a one-path mentality, as in a checkout workflow: There are clear instructions about what to do next after each step.

Other websites might allow some freedom but make suggestions or offer a guided option, as in a tutorial or onboarding experience for a new application. Your product may generate popup suggestions of where to go next, but the user still has control to disregard the suggestion and do what they want.

Both approaches have value, depending on the context, so consider how and where people might need more guidance versus dropping them in and letting them choose where to go next.

User-led vs. site-guided interaction elements may seem similar to one-path vs. many-paths elements. However, each set of interaction elements are independent characteristics of a product that can be combined in different ways:

+ **One path/user-led:** The user can go backwards or forwards through a series of interactions. Consider surveys or shopping carts where the user can jump between next and previous screens.

+ **One path/site-led:** The user must follow a path and cannot go backwards (or can only go backwards in the reverse order).

+ **Many paths/user-led:** The default web experience, where users can go anywhere on a website and access information in any order.

+ **Many paths/site-led:** The user is asked a series of questions about what they want to accomplish. Based on those answers, a unique series of path options are generated for the desired experience.

Impact of Interactions on Brand

Why is a discussion of interactions placed in a chapter on brand?

Interaction is an intimate part of brand. Consider the dreaded trip to the Division of Motor Vehicles. Long lines, unfriendly staff, exacting forms that must be filled out perfectly, or risk being bumped to another wait in another line: These interactions form the brand of the DMV.

In the same way, your product's interactions are crucial to the way people interpret your brand. From site loading time to clear navigation and each widget or form field, the interactions are what make or break your company's brand. Consider some of the guiding words you chose to describe your brand. Do your site interactions clearly align with those words?

Summary

Your brand is a collection of attributes that represent the image and personality of your product or organization. Your brand goes deeper than just colors and logos; it encompasses both tangible and intangible characteristics and can deliver a unique, positive, and consistent experience for your users. As you create your content, products and business, look for opportunities to reinforce your brand identity and evoke positive emotional responses through interactions with your audience.

To create an intentional brand, develop a recognizable tone and voice that reinforces your brand. Apply that tone and voice consistently across all of your communications. Document your branding standards in a brand style guide, and keep the guide updated as your brand evolves. Ensure that all team members and contributors apply the guidelines correctly and consistently. Treat your product's interaction elements as another opportunity to reinforce your brand and demonstrate your commitment to a great user experience.

Put It in Action

Your brand is more than just a logo, so spend some time defining it fully. In your workbook, fill in the brand style guide template with the details of your brand, and use the interaction elements worksheet pages to define the essential guidelines of how you and your team will build your product. When making brand-defining decisions, take some time to review the work you've done and synthesized: How will your brand fit within the market? What resonates with your personas? How can your brand support your company's mission, vision and goals, and your product's value proposition? Reviewing this information will keep your brand aligned and on track for success.

DESIGN

IDEA

PLANNING

Craft Your Content

CHAPTER SIX

Content is most often equated with long pages of text like blog posts or About pages on company websites. But words are everywhere. Like in this book you're reading.

And in the tiny interactions of your product. Content is more than text: icons, images, videos, audio, and GIFs are other types of content included in your product that reflect your brand. You should care about how they are created and what message they are communicating.

Enter content strategy. *Content strategy* is the method by which you determine the content you need, and then create, update, and maintain all of the content within your product or website over time. The sooner you start creating and maintaining a content strategy, the less time and money you'll waste trying to figure out the proper tone, voice, and message required for the next round of updates, or on reworking content that's out of alignment.

> **Note**
> *It may be the case in your organization that others are in charge of your content and, by extension, your content strategy. That's great! Use this chapter as more of a conversation starter with those in charge, so you can get the content (and subsequent strategy and plan) you need for your projects.*

Building a Content Strategy

A content strategy has two main parts, each containing several subsections.

+ Content structure

+ Content governance

These items are all collected and managed in a content style or strategy guide, much like the brand style guide covered in Chapter 5. It's important to keep this document up to date so that anyone creating content can easily follow the most recent guidelines. Let's break down each of these parts.

Content Structure

Content structure focuses on the details of how to create your content. The subcomponents of content structure provide the blueprints for crafting new content and updating current content in a consistent way so, like your brand, your content is always properly representing your organization. Content structure is divided into six sections:

+ Content structure
    - Core content strategy
    - Core message
    - Core personas, ranked
    - Voice and tone table
    - Required content types
    - Content specific to certain audiences or industries, including jargon, imagery, videos, etc.

Core Content Strategy

The *core content strategy* is the main mission statement for your content. It guides you in how to best create and repurpose the content in your product to help meet the organization's goals, as defined in Chapter 1. A core content strategy answers how your content is going to bring you closer to, or help you meet, those goals. Here's an example of a core content strategy:

> *The content will create a friendly, helpful atmosphere, using plain language and simple imagery to keep the product relatable for our wide range of audiences.*

This statement clarifies the overall intent and purpose of the content and will help drive all content decisions. Your content strategy should do the same for your organization.

To keep your content in line across all your web properties, it's important to be clear on your core message. A *core message* is the single most important thing you want people to know after viewing your content. All of your content, from images and icons to text, should echo this message. Slack has a great example of this: Their core message is that they make communication easy and friendly. Throughout their app, they include helpful tips, friendly but professional messages on welcome and loading screens (as seen in Figure 6.1), and bright, cheerful icons and images. No matter where you are in the Slack app, their core message comes through.

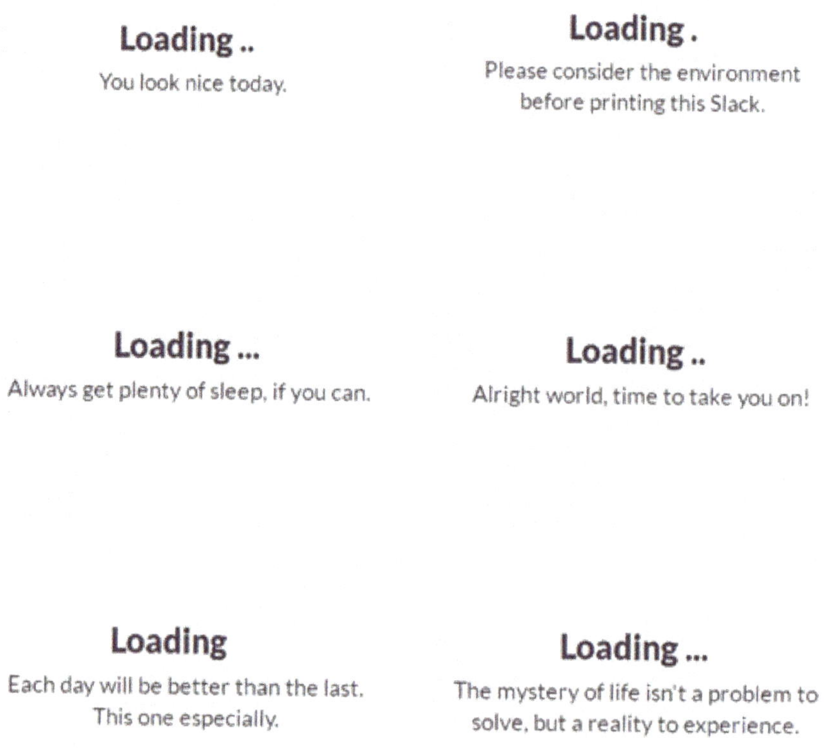

Loading ..

You look nice today.

Loading .

Please consider the environment
before printing this Slack.

Loading ...

Always get plenty of sleep, if you can.

Loading ..

Alright world, time to take you on!

Loading

Each day will be better than the last.
This one especially.

Loading ...

The mystery of life isn't a problem to
solve, but a reality to experience.

Figure 6.1: Engaging loading messages on what could be an annoying or frustrating interface.

Include your personas in your content strategy guide, and rank them according to their importance in the product. This way, the personas are easily referenceable in a contextual way by anyone working on content later on.

Remember that your persona rankings may change depending on context, such as onboarding, or for specific promotions or goals. Be sure to note any allowed deviations in your content strategy guide.

Voice and Tone Table

A *voice and tone table* is a table you fill out to define the attributes of your brand and keep your team in line. The voice and tone table provides structure to creating a personality that will represent your brand and how to write content that reflects those traits. By defining traits, you'll have much more success delivering content with consistency, regardless of who is creating it.

To choose your attributes, first consider your core message, brand, and goals; they will give you some guidance. Then ask yourself and your team, "How would I describe (or want to describe) my company or product if it were a person?" Brainstorm ideas and then determine which attributes best describe your brand. You'll want to choose 2 or 3 traits that complement each other; choosing disparate attributes like "humorous" and "somber" won't really work in combination when it's time to create content.

Once you've identified the attributes you want to focus on, you can fill out a voice and tone table for each trait, as shown in Figure 6.2. The voice and tone table contains the trait, a correct example, an incorrect example, the rationale for why this trait is important, and, if needed, explanation about why one example is correct and one is incorrect.

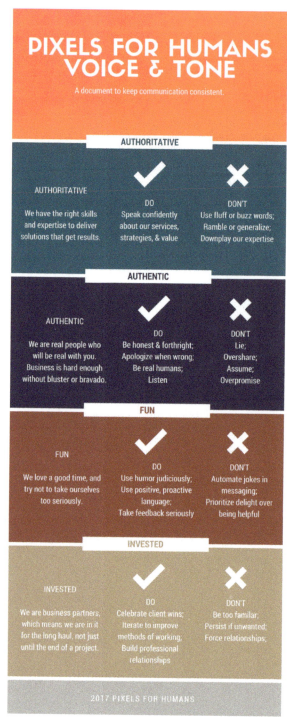

Figure 6.2: Example of a voice and tone table.

For each section of the voice and tone table, consider the following:

+ **What is the attribute you want to convey?** This is the top section, starting with "Your voice is…" To fill this out, consider the appropriate attribute or characterization for your organization. How do you want your users and customers to feel when interacting with you? Write it here.

+ **Write like this:** Provide a short example of content that communicates that attribute to your users. You can create an example or copy one from existing material.

+ **Not like this:** What would not demonstrate the feeling? In this section, show something that could be confused for correct, so it's clear what the boundaries are for the attribute. Again, you can create an example or copy one from existing material.

+ **Why?** This is possibly the most important part of the table. Explain why the feeling is important for your clients and users and the goal for making them feel this way. Relate the "why" back to your brand or to an experience in your product. For example, reduce user anxiety when an error occurs, or increase user confidence that a task is completed appropriately.

You should update your voice and tone table regularly as your brand evolves and your messaging changes, especially as you discover what attributes resonate best with your audiences.

Required Content Types

It's helpful and important to identify all of the different types of content you'll need to create for your product. This will give you a starting to-do list, as well as clarity around the level of effort involved. Your list should specify the context in which different types of content will be used. For images, your list might include:

+ Blog header images   + Team photo images
+ Social media images   + Product images

When you begin creating content, you can add examples of each content type to your content strategy guide for future reference. As always, be sure to update it as needed over time. In the section on content governance below, we'll cover the people involved in creating, editing, and managing these different types of content.

When creating a product, it's important to understand and use language, images, and other content that is specific to your audience's expectations. This way, you are not making your users think too hard. If you use content that does not match your audience's expectation, you are likely to confuse, alienate, or even lose visitors as a result. One obvious example of this is if you were building a checkout cart for an online store, and you called it "reusable bag" instead of "cart," it would definitely cause some confusion; in this example, most people would figure it out, but you could lose customers by deviating from common language and content.

Consider Starbucks as another example. They have a whole language, complete with shorthand and code for all of their specialty beverages. Loyal Starbucks customers learn that language, and have expectations about what their experience will be like. If tomorrow your local Starbucks changed that code by renaming drink sizes "tiny," "so-so," and "huge," customers would feel disconnected and likely frustrated when trying to order their drinks. Instead of making huge changes to existing language, Starbucks adds to it over time by adding new drinks, snacks, and modifications, as well as periodically highlighting existing drinks that might be new to some. In this way, they are able to expand and evolve their content without disruption.

PRO TIP

Don't Reinvent the Wheel

This example of "cart" vs. "reusable bag" is a great case where brand can be taken too far. A company focused on environmental sustainability might well want to rename common interface elements to better reflect their brand. Guide clients away from doing this, especially if this is part of the checkout process. Many users are already anxious about entering their contact and credit card information online. Don't add to that anxiety by eliminating established standards and terminology.

In the same way, by starting with expected and familiar content, you can start to build unique content over time that will blend with the existing content expectations. For example, before Twitter, no one thought that "tweeting" would become a regular business activity. As with all deviations from expectations, just be sure that the reward you provide is worth more than the effort of having to think. We talk about this more in the mental models section of Chapter 7.

Content Governance

Content governance is the strategy for creating and managing your content over time. It includes 3 main sections:

+ Content governance
    - Schedule and workflow for creating, updating, and archiving content
    - People involved and their roles
    - Content audit

A well-designed content governance model addresses the following elements:

+ Time needed to create each content type (generally)

+ Frequency of content creation and updates

+ Number of revisions or edits per update

+ Content owner

+ Content creator

+ Any additional contributors or editors

+ Anyone who needs to provide approval or sign-off

Most of your content will be created in tandem with the creation and updating of your product, so many details will be tied to that and included in any project plans you made (see Chapter 2). Independent content - content that stands alone on its own page and is not tied to a larger design project, like blog posts or landing pages - can be created according to its own schedule, making it easier to manage than content that's part of a larger project, such as error messages and navigation.

Content Schedules/Editorial Calendar

Regardless of the quantity of content you maintain, you'll want to define a schedule for creating, updating, and archiving content, for each type of content you need. This schedule is often referred to as an *editorial calendar.* A editorial calendar will help you determine how often you need to work on your content. Different types of content will have different schedules, and some content may not need to be archived. It's best to coordinate your content schedule with any existing or upcoming projects; this way your content team won't be surprised or unprepared for needed content updates as part of a larger project.

In addition to an overall schedule of content updates, you'll want to create a list of how long each content type takes to create, including the number of editing rounds typically needed. This will allow you to plan effectively when it's time to create new content.

People Involved

As you may expect, the creation of content involves many people, including the content creators, editors, marketing personnel, managers with approval rights, and more. With all these cooks in the kitchen, it's important to keep track of them all and understand each person's role. This information can be added to your project plan or management system to make your content strategy work more efficiently.

There are a few steps to ensuring you've identified all of the necessary content team members. First, and most importantly, ensure that each content object has an owner and a creator. A content owner is responsible for requesting content, receive feedback on it from various editors, keeping it up-to-date, and archiving it if needed. A content creator is responsible for creating the content requested, and making updates to the content as needed, including incorporating feedback. For most content, the owner and creator will be the same person: your content strategist. However, if you don't have a dedicated content strategist, you will need to divide these responsibilities among the team to ensure that content is created intentionally, instead of as an afterthought. One example of where the owner and the creator are not the same person is a blog post. The blog manager is the content owner and is responsible for ensuring that the content is created, edited, and approved at the right times. The author of the post is the content creator, responsible for creating and updating the content according to the schedule.

Next, identify any additional contributors, including editors who will be involved in the content process for each content type. In our blog post example, we may have additional editors, as well as a photographer or graphic designer creating images to support the post content. Additional editors are also very common with marketing materials. Marketing teams often have people specifically focused on editing content to match any marketing requirements, like snippets for social media posts, and should be involved in the process. Be sure that your contributors understand the timeframe they have to complete their roles so they can schedule their time accordingly to avoid bottlenecks.

Finally, identify the stakeholders who will need to provide feedback and approval for your content. Stakeholders might be additional members of your team, your product manager, or your CEO and anyone else who has a say. These people have the power to wreck your plan, your content, and your schedule, so be diligent in communicating expectations and context. Make sure they know what they need to do and by when. While it's possible that you'll still end up behind schedule waiting for approval or feedback, you'll have better luck staying on track the more you communicate.

> **Note**
> *If you're a startup or working with a small team, there may be far fewer people on your team. It may in fact be only you! That's OK. Just do the best you can and as your team grows, revisit your content roles to make sure you're delegating work to support your company's growth.*

Content Audit

A *content audit* is the creation of a list of all your content, where it exists on your website, the URL of the content and what pages link to each piece of content. It's important to do a content audit for your website or product if you've never done one and don't have a list of all your content already created and up-to-date. Even if you have a brand-new product and all your content is completely new, it's important to do periodic content audits. Audits let you assess the specific content you have and determine how to adjust your content strategy, and, by extension, your content. Content is a bit like knick-knacks or lawn furniture: Everything is fine until suddenly your living room is exploding with unused and unwanted stuff. In the same way, your content can get overloaded if you don't do a periodic spring cleaning.

A content audit can be time-consuming, but the process is straightforward: To audit your content, make a note of every page and piece of content that exists in your product or on your website, usually in a spreadsheet. Be sure include microcopy (small bits of text or copy that provide information or instruction, like error messages) and other smaller pieces of content. Go page by page and search for links to pages that exist in only one location. Refer to your manager for additional pages, sections, or content that exists but is not linked.

Once you've finished your content audit, look for ROT: redundant, outdated, and trivial content. Clean out what isn't in line with your current brand, your products and services, or your company direction. Don't repeat the same information in several locations, as this is hard to maintain. Identify and remove meaningless content. Jen grinds her teeth at websites that proudly proclaim, "Welcome to our website!" Of course we are welcome; it's your public website! Think of a more creative way to make visitors feel comfortable.

Doing an audit reveals any content that does not meet your strategy or exists because no one was responsible for it, giving insight into how best to move forward. The good news is that, no matter what's going on with your product, you can create this spreadsheet now and add to it every time new content is added or existing content is removed, to keep it up to date going forward (and if you've been doing this, HIGH FIVE!). Taking stock of your content periodically allows you to keep everything recent and relevant, without old or random content.

Creating Content: Tips and Tricks

Once your strategy is in place, it's time to create some content. Here are some tips and tricks for creating content that works.

Tell Your Story

Stories are everywhere. From cover letters for job applications, to allegories about working in business, to the contextual examples in this book, stories help people make sense of the world in a way that a checklist of information, or *takeaways*, don't. People connect to a story, as they can picture themselves in the situation, so it makes sense that your content should convey information through stories. This may seem odd, especially for a product, but it's easier than you think.

Let's look at an example. We mentioned before that the Slack core message is to be communicative and friendly. The Slack loading screens display conversational, friendly messages that make a more personal connection. The Slack story is conveyed through the messages they choose and the phrasing of their interactions, as shown in Figure 6.3. They extend this further in their app through Slackbot, their system's artificial intelligence (AI) designed to helps users navigate Slack. Slackbot can be customized to give additional responses based on triggers. One company used Slackbot for onboarding, as shown in Figure 6.3.

Figure 6.3: Slackbot configured for company onboarding.

This is part of what keeps people engaged using Slack: the story of a helpful tool just trying to make your day, your work, and your communication a little better and easier.

What elements should you consider when telling your story? Good stories have characters (usually the user; often also your product), motivations, some level of "conflict," and a resolution. For Slack, the characters are you, your team, and Slack (and by extension, Slackbot, as a representative of Slack). The motivations and conflict are tied together: Communication with Slack and the team is both the motivation and the conflict for the characters. The resolution is brought by Slack: being helpful, friendly, and there when needed, as shown in Figure 6.3, and then being quietly in the background when not.

This makes sense, as all products exist in an effort to solve some problem, whether real or perceived. Web products by their very nature have conflict (and hopefully resolution) built in: X is a problem that we can solve. By building this out into more of a story, you can meet people where they are and foster more, and better, engagement. To build out your product's story, just get your ideas on paper; walk through it from step to step. What's the problem? How do people feel about the problem now and how do they work around or overcome it? How can you make that easier or better for them? What is the end benefit or result? Those questions will give you the structure for your story; then you can weave the story throughout your product.

Iterate

Once you have your basic story down, and your first drafts of content created, *iterate*. When you iterate, you consider other ways of saying the same thing, or other images or icons that might communicate the same ideas. Try several ways until you find what works, similar to defining your purpose for ethnographic interviews, as discussed in Chapter 3. When iterating, do it in context whenever possible; you may think an image or icon is a good fit while searching stock sites, but when put in context of where it will be used, it might not work as expected.

Another useful technique to help you iterate successfully is to read your content out loud and see how it sounds. Does it sound natural? Easy? Approachable? Or does it sound stilted and awkward? Reading your content aloud helps you find the final spots where your content just isn't quite there yet, and confirm that the good content is good.

One good example of the importance of context in your iterations is from a recent student of Heather's. She had designed a landing page for her company's product and created a headline she thought would resonate with the target audience. However, when she tested the headline, she found that the participants didn't understand the message when asked to explain it. She was able to test a few more versions before finding a version that was really successful in communicating what her audience needed to hear.

Edit

Similar to iterating is editing: Instead of trying new things, refine what's close to working or that conveys the right idea. One rule of web editing is to cut your content. Then cut it again. Most people use more words than needed to say something; by forcing yourself to be brief, you'll end up with clearer, more digestible content. This means your customers will know they are in the right place sooner; they'll understand your value more quickly; and they'll appreciate that they didn't have to work so hard to figure it all out.

Test Your Content

Testing your content helps you understand what is and is not resonating with your audiences. Some good tests for content effectiveness are 5-second tests, A/B split tests, and in-depth content tests. Let's break down each test:

+ **5-second tests:** In this test, you show a test participant your product or website for 5 seconds, and then remove it. After you've removed the website or product from their view, ask the participant the following questions:
  - What do you think the website is for?
  - What stood out to you about the website?

  You may also want to ask for their impressions of what the brand was about. This helps you understand what first impressions you are making.

+ **A/B split tests:** As the name implies, this test involves splitting your product into two versions, A and B, and testing which version performs better over time. In addition to testing different content, you can also test different designs, different offers, and more. This test is easy to set up, by creating two versions and then serving them up to your audience at random.

+ **In-depth content tests:** If you have a content-heavy website, such as WebMD, you'll want to test the comprehensive nature of the content itself. Can people understand it? Does it fulfill its intended purpose? By conducting an in-depth test of your content, you can determine the answers to these questions. The test itself is simple: Ask participants to read through the content thoroughly, navigate them away from the page, and then ask them to answer detailed questions that require some comprehension of content.

Summary

Content is more than words. Images, GIFs, videos, audio clips, icons, and UI labels are all forms of content that need to be considered and chosen intentionally. Create your product's content deliberately, in a way that supports your organizational strategy, product goals, and brand identity by developing a content strategy.

Your content strategy should capture your ideal content structure and defines your content governance model. Enforce your content strategy. Ensure that all content contributors are aware of, and work in accordance with, your strategy.

For more details about the pieces of content strategy, check out this foundational post by the folks at Brain Traffic:

http://braintraffic.com/blog/brain-traffic-lands-the-quad

Put It in Action

Build on your brand style guide with a content style guide and editorial calendar. To start, fill out the content style guide template found in the workbook. You'll define the core content strategy and message, referring to your business mission and purpose, as well as the value proposition and plan for your product. Fill in and update the details from your created personas and brand guide's voice and tone table. List all content types you know of right now, but be prepared to revisit this as you build your product. You may discover content types you didn't realize you'd need, as well as content types you actually don't need. Finally identify all the people involved in the process on a regular basis (do not include content creators for things like guest posts or one-off content pieces; those will be included in your editorial calendar).

Use the template provided in the workbook to create an editorial calendar of your content. Be sure to include both recurring content (like blog posts, social media updates and similar items) and product specific content (like headlines, static site pages, microcopy and similar items). As possible, note the people involved for each piece of content. If it's your typical team, you can abbreviate to save space.

Finally, use the linked template from the workbook to track your content and do an audit if needed. As you create new content, track it there and periodically review existing content to test, update, or archive content as needed.

IDEA

DESIGN

Organize Your Information

CHAPTER SEVEN

"Information Architecture is the way we arrange the parts of something to make it understandable."

— Abby Covert, *How to Make Sense of Any Mess*

The internet is primarily a tool of communication and information. Everything on the internet must be organized to convey that information. Whether the intent is to inform, to engage, or to allow action, all of that information needs to be arranged in a way that meets both the goals of the business, and the people using it. When architecting a building, room placement and layout are considered heavily. The same idea applies on the web. There are numerous ways to arrange the information on any given website though. How do you decide which approach is best? It depends.

LinkedIn is a good example of the complexity that architecting information on a website can bring. As you can see, the LinkedIn website has at least three different areas of navigation (the top bar, the drop-down panel, and the "footer" content in the sidebar), as well as numerous other "hotspots" of action, which we've identified in red. That's a lot! And LinkedIn knows it. These groupings of navigational elements didn't happen by chance; they were organized in this way intentionally.

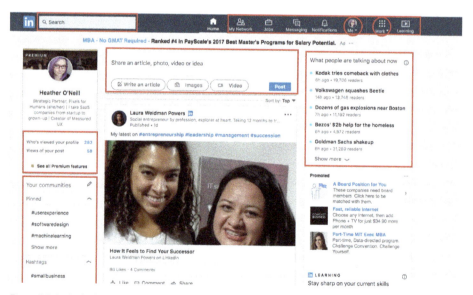

Figure 7.1: LinkedIn has a ridiculous amount of navigation on their site.

Despite the intentional organization, LinkedIn's navigation doesn't meet the mark. One of the chief complaints about the LinkedIn website is that it's almost impossible to find anything aside from the main feed. Because of its complexity, it's hard to find a solution that really allows a majority of LinkedIn users to find and get what they need easily. With so many things going on, creating a website structure for LinkedIn that makes sense is a daunting task. They need an information architecture.

Information architecture (IA) is all about making sense of the information on the web by intentionally considering the information, and taking the time to assemble it in a logical or intuitive way. The thing is, "intuitive" websites are only intuitive for some people, even if it's a majority of people. There will always be outliers. Different people have different mental models, which can often be contradictory.

Mental Models and the MAYA Principle

Mental models are the assumptions people have about how something will work, based on their past experiences and understanding. These assumptions, whether conscious or unconscious, inform a person's expectations when interacting with the web. A great example of this is early website design. Early on, website designs relied heavily on *skeuomorphism* – the process of making web items resemble real-world items to help people connect the digital to the real world. Later, *flat design*, where design elements are two-dimensional or "flat" in appearance, grew in prominence and popularity. Even the use of a physical folder as the icon for where to store computer files takes a cue from people's mental models.

Mental models aren't something you can prescribe or instantly create. Instead, you need to identify them through the use of cognitive empathy, which helps you shape conversations with your audience in order to gather and understand the right information. *Cognitive empathy* helps you understand people's expectations based on personal understanding and experiences, i.e., their mental models. In most cases, the mental models for your audience are informed by other, more popular websites.

For example, if you're designing an e-commerce site, you may want to model your shopping cart experience after a large online retailer, such as Amazon. At the very least, you'll want to understand the Amazon process and why it works before you decide to deviate from it. The value proposition of any significant deviation must be very compelling because you're risking the chance of people getting frustrated and abandoning their carts. In short, change is hard, so to get people on board with changes, there has to be a lot of additional value or they will feel frustrated and may not even bother. This leads into a concept know as *most advanced yet acceptable*, or MAYA.

The principle of MAYA is the idea that advancements need to happen in incremental stages to be adopted broadly and successfully. Compare the earliest iPhones to the latest ones, and you'll see the changes that happened after people became accustomed to using a smartphone. This is why Blackberry devices were popular in the early 2000s but then tapered off. Blackberry's design worked within the bounds of what people were already comfortable with in the 2000s – a physical keypad. However, as smartphones evolved and keypads moved to become more digital instead of physical, Blackberry's keypad didn't. Blackberry quickly became outdated and while they filled a middle ground with their initial smartphone designs, they lost momentum by failing to advance.

Another good example of MAYA is Google Glass, the 2013 wearable technology that allowed people to access applications like email, websites and photos through a pair of glasses. Google Glass was a huge departure from all other wearables at that time (like Fitbits), shipping with its own operating system, a laundry list of features, and an API for third party developers. In short, it was a complex technology in a very different and new package. Because Google Glass looked and functioned like a complex piece of technology, it was unrelatable to the general public, and it caused a number of uncomfortable social interactions before it was pulled from the market in 2015. Snapchat Spectacles, released in 2016 and now on their second version, look like cheap but trendy sunglasses, and came with a simple premise: They record videos and take pictures. That's it. Snapchat Spectacles combines a few simple tasks people are familiar with into something that makes sense and feels like a natural extension of an existing product, instead of a complicated new tool with more success in the market. That's MAYA in action.

On the web, mental models and the MAYA principle mean that you shouldn't completely reinvent very common patterns or new ways of organizing your information, especially not without providing significant, tangible value. Even if the new pattern is better, if people can't get the connection and see the value immediately, they won't want the update. Humans are resistant to change, so a paradigm shift takes time. Understanding your audiences' mental models and working from them as a base point for architecting your information will result in a much better product.

Architecting Information

Now that we've established the importance of intentionally organizing your product's information, let's talk about how. There are three main steps to organizing information:

1. Identify the information

2. Define relevant goals and mental models

3. Arrange information and make connections

You may not need all of these steps every time, and some steps are likely to overlap or happen "out of order." This is normal. Also, it's okay if things are fuzzy or nebulous for a while; that's a normal state until you put everything together with design. And don't be surprised if you make more changes once you've put it all together. Seeing things in context always provides additional insight. Ultimately, this will help you figure out the structure of the pages and information in your website and how your navigation will be organized and displayed. It's also helpful if you're reorganizing or adding new features.

To successfully organize your website, you first need to know what it is that you're organizing. Make a list of elements or, if you've already done a content audit from Chapter 6, use the content inventory to get you started. For simple websites, like a personal portfolio, this list might be fairly small: recent work, skills, experience, resume, published articles or books, speaking engagements, and other personal details, like hobbies, working style, or goals. For LinkedIn, which we looked at earlier, the list is much bigger:

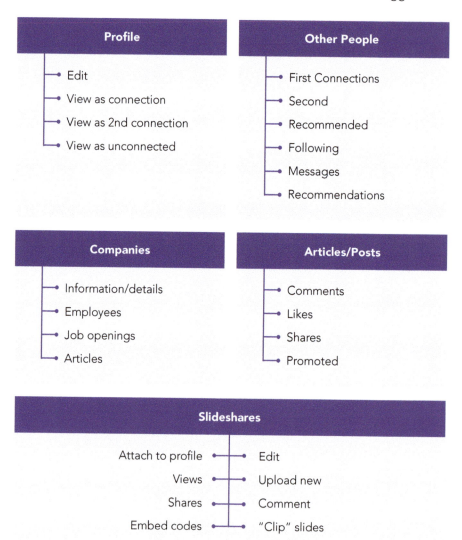

Profile
- Edit
- View as connection
- View as 2nd connection
- View as unconnected

Other People
- First Connections
- Second
- Recommended
- Following
- Messages
- Recommendations

Companies
- Information/details
- Employees
- Job openings
- Articles

Articles/Posts
- Comments
- Likes
- Shares
- Promoted

Slideshares
- Attach to profile
- Views
- Shares
- Embed codes
- Edit
- Upload new
- Comment
- "Clip" slides

That's only a very partial, high-level list. You'll notice that a lot of the sections overlap with other sections, and there are many connections that could be made throughout the list. That's okay at this stage.

The key here is to identify everything you need to convey (information) or allow (action), so in future steps you can organize elements, identify any redundancies (and decide when that's okay), and understand how people are most likely interacting with everything. For now, just list everything that comes to mind. When you're done, leave it alone for a day and then revisit the list; it's likely that you missed some things that you'll think of later. Add those items, even if they seem redundant. And don't be afraid to add things as you go; this list is not meant to be final. It's simply a place to capture every potential element so your final IA will be comprehensive.

Another way to add to your list is use existing language and terminology or competitors' products as a cross reference. Viewing and including competitors' categories will give you a clear sense of how your own terminology fits into the overall market. You can also research Google Trends, Google's site for researching how often different terms are searched compared to all searches. Use Trends to find keywords related to your information; this will give you additional terms to consider and will help when you start organizing your information.

Define Relevant Goals and Mental Models

Now that you have identified relevant information and actions, it's time to organize. How do you organize it in a way that's going to work for those using your product? Start by referencing your personas. In the persona template we provided, there's a section for both goals and mental models. Working from the most important persona downward, list all of the goals and mental models for your audiences. Then go back to your business and project plans: What goals does the organization have? What goals exist for the the product? Lay all of those items out together. Note where the mental models overlap, and identify any areas of conflicting models or goals.

Next, review your research about your competitors: What experiences are they offering to your potential visitors? What common patterns should you be considering for your website, to match your visitors' expectations? What cues can you give users to help them know that they've come to the right place? Write this down as well.

All this information is the context that you will use to inform your organizational choices

Arrange Information and Make Connections

Having done a competitor analysis and researched Google Trends, you know what your audience is expecting and what you want to get out of your product. Using the data that you've gathered, it's time to organize the information on your website, and create your taxonomy. A *taxonomy* is the list of pages and sections of your product, including those explicitly stated in navigation and those linked via other pages or direct URL. Here's what to do:

1. **Visualize your information.** Put all of the information (such as navigation, site topics, content types, features, functionality and other details you plan to include in your product) you need to organize on to sticky notes (or into a Trello board, which is a free digital tool that allows you to group sticky-note-like cards fluidly) and put them on the wall.

2. **Create a base arrangement.** The easiest way to do this is to organize it similarly to your competition; this is a starting point, so don't worry too much if you don't have individual or unique mappings for each item. Just get a general organizational structure in place.

3. **Adjust your organization.** Using Google Trends data, mental models, card sort results, persona and product goals, and any other relevant information, consider what in the current arrangement should change, and how. Move the sticky notes around until something starts to make sense. (Note: It's acceptable and common for items to exist in more than one location. To represent duplicates, just create an extra sticky note of the same item, or use arrows to show relationships.) This might start to look similar to a site map or taxonomy, but most likely it will look more muddled than that (by design). This is the full structure of your website, so it doesn't need to be stripped down.

4. **Refine and finalize.** Take a look at your organizational goals again. Are there any final adjustments you should make based on that information? Review these adjustments with others, especially stakeholders, to get any last feedback and answer any questions about why you chose this organizational structure.

5. **Create a definitive site taxonomy and navigation using your structure.** Taking the organizational structure and hierarchy you created in the previous steps, decide how that will function on your site. Specify the actual navigation items (including the title for each) and then list what can be found in each section. Also note any deep links that will be available on the site, but won't be accessible from the primary navigation. If needed, define a secondary navigation, such as a footer navigation.

The good news about creating an information architecture is that it can be done with a group using the KJ method, explained in Chapter 10, or solo, depending on which approach makes sense for your organization. An information architecture also gives you direct insight into the content you'll need to assemble or create to make this a reality; you can then double check your content list to see if you've missed anything.

Summary

Information architecture is about structuring the content, workflows and organization of your website. Arrange your information in a logical, consistent way that supports your users' goals and your own business goals. Consider mental models and apply cognitive empathy to understand how people search for, consume, and respond to information. Don't reinvent patterns and organizational structures that have proven success without a compelling reason. Relying on established, familiar patterns can help users jump right in and start using your product successfully. Help users along their path by clarifying next steps, connection points, overlaps, and dependencies.

Put It in Action

An information architecture is your first step toward a well-organized, easy-to-use product and shouldn't be overlooked in favor of creating designs or wireframes. In the workbook, follow the steps to start your information architecture. First, list all elements of your product, using your content audit or repository as a starting point. Be sure to capture anything upcoming or in progress that will need a place. Then review your personas and competitor analyses to understand the perspectives your audience has and what they've already seen. Finally, start organizing your information, making connections and grouping items that make sense. Note your final architecture in the workbook, and be prepared to adjust it as you learn more or get feedback from your customers.

IDEA

DESIGN

Create Your Wireframes

In the last several chapters, you've created goals, personas, competitive analyses, branding, content, and information architecture for your product.

How do all of these elements come together to interact with each other on a screen? Wireframing is the process by which the thinking and planning you've done so far becomes tangible.

A *wireframe* is a representation of a screen (or a portion of a screen) that depicts the layout of content elements. Unlike a visual mockup, a wireframe is typically a low-fidelity artifact, meaning that it's not supposed to look very much like the final product visually. Think of it like a blueprint; it shows the skeleton or structure of what you're creating. A wireframe is very effective at conveying the information hierarchy of the page – what content elements, in which arrangement, best serve the page's intended purpose.

In general, wireframing happens before visual design. Color, typography, and imagery are not the focus; you'll address those later. Wireframes are about the content and functionality of the interface.

Ugly Wireframes Work Best

A wireframe's mission in life is to enable product creators to do two things:

+ Focus on content and hierarchy without being distracted by look and feel
+ Make changes quickly based on feedback

While your impulse may be to make everything look beautiful, this can severely undermine the purpose of your wireframes. Stakeholders and users (and even you!) tend to zero in on color and font choices and other graphical elements, while what you need at this stage is feedback on the content and functionality. To avoid distraction and get the feedback you need, make your wireframes look rough, unfinished, and "ugly."

When you share, test, or demo something that so obviously isn't a final design, users and stakeholders will give you feedback that's more relevant, without worrying about wasting time or hurting your feelings (yes, this is a concern!). And you, in turn, will be able to implement that feedback and test the next iteration quickly without agonizing over getting the pixels perfect.

Wireframe Examples

Figure 8.1 shows the style of a typical wireframe, created with a wireframing tool called Balsamiq. It's a wireframe from one of Heather's early clients, focused on self-led online learning.

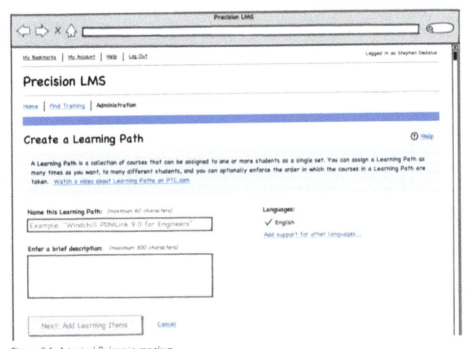

Figure 8.1: A typical Balsamiq mockup.

This wireframe example contains no bold branding or slick graphics, and even the font is Comic Sans! The look is deliberately hand-drawn, even though it was created with sophisticated wireframing software. It's basic black and white, with two shades of blue used sparingly to convey specific kinds of information. Clearly, this is far from what a user would see if they visited the real website in a browser.

With the visual niceties stripped away, what does this wireframe communicate? You can look at it and easily identify the following functional characteristics:

+ It's an interface for creating a learning path.

+ It's asking for two pieces of information: a name and a description.

+ You can choose your language, or add support for another language.

+ There's a link to a video so you can get help with the interface.

The purpose of the page comes to the forefront. This wireframe, along with a few other screens similar to it demonstrating the interactions, could be used to test how well this interface serves the page's purpose. Can the site's users easily understand how to create a learning path?

What if it turns out they cannot? Then you can quickly and easily change anything on this page. Add another field, change the maximum number of characters, or make the help more obvious: You can make the change in a few clicks.

Wireframes like this tend to have little or no functionality or application logic built in; they're far below the level of real software or even a prototype. A user might be able to click on the "Next: Add Learning Items" button and view the next screen, but they won't necessarily be able to actually type anything into the text fields to see how that works, or to see that there's an error message displayed when a field's input is invalid.

However, these wireframes do have enough information in them to support a usability test, which you'll learn about in the next chapter.

Figure 8.2 shows the wireframe for a mobile phone application, featuring a carousel. To demonstrate what the frames of the carousel might look like, the wireframes are shown as four separate screens. The user would be able to slide and see each screen individually.

Figure 8.2: Demonstration of different frames of a carousel in wireframe format.

In this case, the wireframe shows different potential states of an element in the product. This is a good way to test the content in the carousel panels for impact, for showing the flow from panel to panel, or for testing to determine whether a user would choose to interact with the carousel at all.

Creating Effective Wireframes

When you sit down to create wireframes using your tool of choice (see the end of this chapter for ideas), what should you consider? Here are some suggestions based on UX best practices and our experience.

What Should I Include in my Wireframe?

It depends. What are you using it to communicate, and to whom? There are as many answers to this question as there are design projects in the world, but a few common scenarios are worth noting:

+ **Usability testing an interface.** Wireframes are often a great way to run some quick tests with users early on before final design or implementation have begun. See if your users can complete a task using the interface you've designed for them, and get some feedback before it's set for this release. You'll learn how to test your designs in the next chapter. Your wireframes can include as much or as little detail as necessary to allow a user to succeed.

+ **Content and functionality review.** Chances are that you're not the only person involved in building your product. You may have writers, content strategists, and other stakeholders who care about the written copy on the page. And you may have a development team who ask, early on, "What happens when a user clicks this button?" so they can add that to their development backlog. Wireframes are good for defining the core structure of those elements, without worrying too much about presentation. We recommend using real copy (not filler text) as much as possible in wireframes, even if it's only draft copy. This way you'll have a clear sense about how the copy will fit within the page and if the page organization and structure supports it.

+ **Generating layout ideas.** A wireframe can help you get unstuck when you're faced with the dreaded blank canvas. If you know that your page probably needs a pile of photos, some short headline text, and some longer descriptive text, create a wireframe with rough, simplified representations of all of those elements, and then rearrange them on the page until you find a layout that's promising. It's a handy way to brainstorm, even if the only person you're brainstorming with is yourself.

Wireframing Approaches

We recommend taking the following approaches to designing your wireframes for best results.

Start With the Smallest Screens

Mobile-first is a design philosophy popularized by Luke Wroblewski that calls for web practitioners to design for small screens (and other typical mobile-device constraints) first. The constraint of a small screen forces you to prioritize only the information that is truly important, and display it in a format that makes sense for a mobile device user. That prioritization in turn informs what should go on the screen once you scale up to a tablet-sized or desktop-sized display. Those larger types of devices could display more information on the screen, or they could contain the same limited information but arranged differently. Which is better? That depends on the needs of your users, as well as your own strategic priorities. Run some usability tests to find out what works.

Think in a Grid

Imagine your interface divided into 12 equal columns as pictured in Figure 8.3. To create unique sections and page layouts, combine or group some of the columns to create larger columns of different widths for your design. For example, you can make two groupings of six, three groupings of four, a group of three, then six, then three more... the list goes on. Create as many rows of groupings on a page as you need. Each row can have different numbers of column groupings. This is how grid-based layout works.

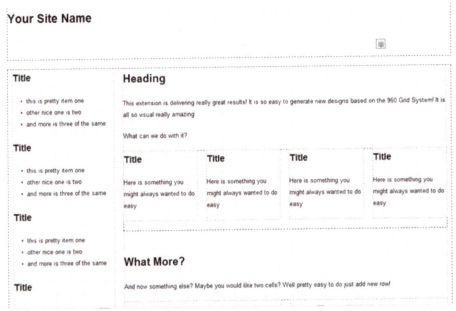

Figure 8.3: An example of how a grid can provide structure to a screen layout.

Grids are fundamental to modern web design. They are the heart of responsive design frameworks like Bootstrap, Foundation, and Ulkit. They're the focus of other frameworks like Susy. And of course, you can code your own grid framework fairly easily!

If you create your wireframes based on a grid system, any designers and developers you collaborate with will thank you later. You will have made it much easier for them to convert your ideas into a successful, well-structured interface.

Be Consistent, and Be Modular

Introduce a few standards to your wireframes and use them consistently. For example, are "read more" links at the end of a blurb formatted as buttons or text links? Are titles aligned to the left or are they centered? When a user is taking a certain action in your product, is a Cancel button always available, or is it never available?

If your screens contain certain components that are repeated often, it's good practice to design these smaller "modules" with the same attention you give to the whole page. This helps you figure out different variations of the component that you'll need, and to be consistent with them. Let's say you have a frequently used component in a sidebar – for example, a list of suggested blog posts. Should there be three posts excerpts with a "read more" link for additional reading, or four posts? Should the excerpts include small thumbnail images or not? What happens if the title of the blog post gets very long? What if some posts have images, while others do not?

This is when it becomes valuable to consider your overall design system. A *design system* is a collection of reusable components, guided by clear standards, that can be assembled together to build any number of applications. In his book *Atomic Design*, Brad Frost provides a great mindset shift to help you get started: Your product is not a series of pages. Instead, it's like a set of building blocks – like LEGO bricks – that can be combined into many different arrangements to achieve different effects. The appearance and behavior of all these building blocks – some simple, like a form field, and some complex, like a navigation bar – make up your design system.

Having a design system allows your product's look and feel and usability to stay consistent when the set of components on a large desktop screen has to be drastically rearranged to work on an iPhone 5 screen. To create your design system, start by looking at a full-page wireframe or mockup. What component parts can you break any give page down into? Those are the pieces of your design system. And the sooner you start thinking of your product as a system of modular pieces, the easier it will be for your whole team to create and adapt new and existing parts of your product, consistently.

The "right" way to design these modular pieces and your overall product will depend on your users and what they understand. Consistently applied standards, captured in your design system, will make it easier for users to navigate and understand your content, no matter what size, shape or format it takes. As an added bonus, this type of consistency will also simplify the development and maintenance of your product.

Have One Focal Point

Look around at websites you admire and web-based tools you use frequently (perhaps for online shopping or banking). There is typically a single major area of focus. On sales-oriented sites, it's the primary headline, featured promotion, or "hero" image. For a bank, it's the single type of transaction you're performing on a given page, like depositing a check. This is the focal point of that particular page.

Then there's the supporting material. Look around the edges of the web page: You'll see the site identity, navigation bar, footer menu, copyright statement, and privacy policy, among other elements. There might be a big sidebar or another page area with many kinds of additional content.

You know those flashy ads and pop-overs you hate, that get in the way on almost every major news site? They are breaking the principle of the single focal point. Your supporting material should do just that: *support* the focus of the page, not distract from it.

Figure 8.4. An illustration on the topic of content focus, by Brad Frost. http://bradfrost.com/ blog/post/7-habits-of-highly-effective-media-queries/

Use Existing Patterns

Everyone wants to be unique, but let's face it: There's virtually no reason for you to reinvent a web interface from scratch. Remix and customize to make your design your own, but first, take advantage of the work others have already done to establish good patterns – patterns that users have come to expect.

Does your website contain a large number of products for your users to browse through? You probably want to let users narrow their search by certain characteristics. Clothing sites like L.L.Bean and appliance sites like Sears use UI techniques that have a lot in common. How could you use a pattern similar to Figure 8.5 on your site?

Whether you're shopping for a refrigerator at Sears (left) or for women's shirts at L.L.Bean (right), a filtering sidebar lets you quickly focus on the most important characteristics and reduce the number of options to explore. Many websites use this pattern, and if your content fits the bill, you should use it too. Remember that the most usable interface is one that the user is already familiar with.

Figure 8.5: Sears filter choices for purchasing a refrigerator (left panel). LLBean filter choices for purchasing women's clothing (right panel)

Wireframing Tools

There are a number of tools – both digital and physical – available to help you create wireframes, to support the way you work best.

Pencil and Paper (or Whiteboard and Marker)

In the simplest method, grab a pencil and some paper, and draw your interface. There's no programming involved and no software to learn – just draw, erase, and redraw. It could be argued that these are not "professional" looking, since they're hand-drawn. However, sometimes these types of wireframes are the most effective, as they're very fast to create and it's clear to everyone that changes are super-simple to make.

When working with a team on solving particularly challenging problems, it may make sense to sketch your wireframe ideas on a whiteboard. This method allows real time design collaboration, similar to pair programming, and can stimulate new ideas and solutions.

Software You Already Know

Are you a fan of Adobe Photoshop, Illustrator, or InDesign? Sketch or Canva? Microsoft PowerPoint or Word – or some other program that supports drawing? Any of these tools can be used to make wireframes, and if you're already well versed in the software, you can get a lot done with no learning curve. This is especially helpful if you only need to make a few screens or convey a general idea. If you have a complex set of wireframes that you plan to revisit over time, then wireframing-specific software is worth your time to learn.

Software Meant for Wireframing

There are many tools and products available that are specifically designed for creating wireframes. There are dozens of possibilities, with all different types of advantages and disadvantages. Popular tools include:

+ **Standalone software packages that run on your computer:** Balsamiq, OmniGraffle, Adobe XD, Axure RP, MockPlus

+ **Software as a service or web-based tools:** Wireframe.cc, Moqups

+ **Software as a service, where wireframing is one aspect of the software:** UXPin, InVision

Wireframing tools have several advantages over pencil and paper or software that you're already proficient in:

+ **They contain patterns for frequently used web interface elements.** For example, they give you the ability to quickly and easily draw a navigation bar, a box for an image, a button, an image carousel, form fields, and so much more.

+ **Many tools allow you to link one wireframe to another.** In other words, when your user clicks a button, you can easily program a link or button on one wireframe to jump to another wireframe. No special skills are required to link it up.

Of course, you'll need to weigh these benefits against the drawback of having to learn another software program – one that you may not need to use that often. And there's the cost of the software: You'll want to evaluate what kind of payment structure best fits your needs (typically either a one-time purchase or a recurring subscription). Fortunately, most products allow you to try them for free to see what works best for you.

Summary

Before you begin the development phase, create wireframes that represent the visual layout of screens or content elements. These wireframes are the point at which all your work starts coming together. As simple sketches of interfaces, interactions, and page layouts, wireframes allow you to quickly try various solutions.

Wireframes can be done by anyone. No design knowledge needed – just grab a Sharpie and some blank paper, because ugly wireframes work best! Keep the focus on content elements, hierarchy, and functionality, and not on visual design elements. You can also use your wireframes as a basis for usability testing or developing your product.

Put It in Action

While there are no templates in the workbook, creating your first wireframe is just a matter of going for it. Using your IA , existing content, and understanding of the market, competitors and your personas, create a few sketches of what your product could look like, using your favorite tool. Iterate on these initial wireframes by getting feedback from your stakeholders and colleagues, and through usability testing, as outlined in the next chapter.

IDEA VALIDATION

DESIGN VALIDATION

Test Your Interactions

CHAPTER NINE

Usability testing is a process of asking target audience representatives to try to do certain predefined tasks on your website.

While they attempt the tasks, you observe them and ask questions about their thought process and decision making to understand their mental models, and to identify areas of your site that meet or don't support those mental models. Usability testing helps you confirm that you've chosen the correct patterns and interactions, or, more frequently, helps identify where you've missed the mark.

Usability testing also helps you understand why something is happening. In tracking analytics, as described in Chapter 10, you might notice that 90% of people abandon their shopping carts halfway through check out. Although you know that this is happening, you don't know why. Usability testing helps you identify why something is a problem, and provides insights into how to fix it (as well as what not to fix).

Do I Really Need to Usability Test?

"But there are lots of patterns out there and best practices. If I just use those, I should be fine. Right?" Yes and mostly no. Best practices are best only in certain contexts. Patterns, while useful, generally do not cover all of the interactions your product needs, so you'll need to think about the spaces between patterns that link different patterns together. Some patterns might not be possible because of complexity, data, budget, or other reasons, meaning you'll need to come up with an alternative. Therefore, testing is important and should be done regularly.

Major organizations, including Amazon, Google, and Apple, conduct testing, so you'll be in good company.

While there's no hard and fast rule about the timing for usability testing, there are a few guidelines to consider when setting your cadence for usability testing.

+ **Team Size** – If you have a small team or only one person doing research, there's a hard limit on how much testing you actually can do. Be patient and work on building up your longterm database of customer insights.

+ **Other Existing Feedback or Research Efforts** – Similarly, if you or your research team are spending time conducting other research or collecting feedback in other ways, this may limit your time. You can also try to maximize on these efforts by combining them (a great way to do this is to end a shorter usability test with a mini customer interview).

+ **Current Design and Development Process and Release Cycles** – If you're working in 2 week sprints, it may make sense to test 1 – 2 users per sprint. If you're working on smaller sprints within larger milestones, you may want to test only once or twice per milestone, to keep the team moving. Use your existing processes to help guide you to a testing schedule that makes sense.

+ **Access to Customers or Potential Customers** – It's great to do a lot of testing, but you need access to a lot of people to do so. If you only have a small customer base or your audience is harder to reach, testing less often will help you from wearing out people.

+ **Stage/Maturity of Product or Feature Being Tested** – While every iteration of a product should be tested, if your product is newer, more testing earlier will help you launch something that's going to be more successful for less effort. For established or legacy products that are getting small updates, you can use a less frequent testing schedule.

If you're not sure, a good starting point that Usability Testing expert Steve Krug recommends is to do a round of usability testing once a month. We echo that here and add that if you're working on multiple concurrent projects, each project should get its own round of testing each month. After a few months, you can decide if that cadence is working for you or if you need to adjust your testing.

Basics of Usability Testing

A usability test typically involves several key components:

+ An application, website, or prototype

+ A testing goal

+ Several members of each target audience you want to test

+ Common or expected tasks for each audience

+ Scenarios created from those tasks

+ One facilitator and several observers

+ Software for screen sharing and recording (as needed)

+ A testing script and interview questions

As you might suspect, you'll be best served by capturing all this information in a planning document; we've provided a template as part of your workbook. Here's a breakdown of each component.

Application, Website, or Prototype

This one probably seems obvious; you can't run a test without having something to test. However, what is less obvious is that you don't need to have a fully functioning, fully completed product or prototype in order to test. You can test with as little as:

+ Your competitor's product (assuming it's free or they offer a free trial)

+ Your current (not yet finalized) product

+ A low-fidelity clickable prototype, hot-linked wireframes, or PDF

+ A paper sketch or printed wireframes of your product.

Any of these are sufficient to conduct a usability test. And because each becomes available at different points in a project, you can get feedback throughout each point of your creative process.

Just as we covered the importance of setting business and project goals, it's also important to have a goal for your usability testing that states what you want to find out from the testing. Here are a few example testing goals that might apply if you were building a project management app:

+ Discover any points where the scheduling flow is confusing or breaks down.

+ Test the experience of the new sharing functionality

+ Find out why users fail to successfully share documents through the app

As you can see, these goals are all focused on discovering information. The last goal in particular is of note because there's an implicit statement that we know about a problem – users start sharing documents but don't complete the share successfully – but we don't know why that's happening, so we're testing to find out.

To create a testing goal, reference your project, user and business goals to determine what you need to find out in order to make the right design changes. A goal keeps your testing focused, and drives the structure of the test, as well as determining the best participants and scenarios.

PRO TIP

Always test your wireframes

Testing your wireframes with your well-defined audience provides immediate value:

+ **It's trivial to change a wireframe.** Wireframing software is designed to allow you to make quick and easy changes. You don't have to change a database structure or recode a form, which is much more difficult, time-consuming, and costly.

+ **Wireframes are not the finished product.** Clients and stakeholders often won't give feedback on what they think is a final or finished product. They are usually worried about how much it would cost to change it. You will get more honest feedback with a wireframe, making your product that much better.

+ **You can test a pile of wireframes quickly.** Changing code, debugging it, and testing takes much longer than changing a few wireframes.

The right people are another obvious necessity for usability testing. It's important to make sure you have people lined up to participate in your test (hereafter referred to as participants). The goal you set (and the overall project goal) will tell you which persona or personas you are focused on understanding. However, recruiting the right participants can be a bit of a struggle; it's not always easy or even possible to get time from your target personas. So how do you overcome this challenge? Several things can help you get the right people in the room:

+ **Offer the right incentive.** For monetary offerings, be sure to offer an amount commensurate with the value of the person's time. It's embarrassing to offer someone who makes $100 per hour a $10 incentive; that's not actually an incentive at that point and you'll find it hard to get people willing to participate. On the other hand, $10 may be sufficient if you are targeting high school or college students.

  For non-monetary compensation, you'll need to evaluate each case at the time. Lawyers may not want cash but they might be interested in referrals for future clients. Other specialties may accept an analysis of their product in exchange for their time. You may even be able to find folks who are motivated to make your product better, so they're happy to give you the time without compensation. Just be sure you compensate people as you are able, so you don't use up all your audience's goodwill.

  In some instances, no amount of compensation of any kind will make a difference. One common example of this is doctors: They have little to no free time as it is, so there's very little you could offer to make it worth their while. Depending on what you are testing, it's often okay to use a proxy, such as a physician's assistant, nurse, medical student, or personal assistant. While the proxies aren't the direct end users, they are likely the closest you'll be able to reasonably get to a doctor, unless the doctor has a vested interest in your product.

+ **Use a recruiting company.** This sounds costly, but it can save you on time and effort, which, if left unchecked, can ultimately make your testing cost more. Any worthwhile recruiting company will know the audiences they can and cannot reach and will be upfront about what you can expect. Working with a recruiting company can be helpful if you're working on tight timelines or having trouble reaching the right audiences.

+ **Reach out to your network.** Often you can find a connection to audiences that, while not exactly hard to reach, are less likely to proactively volunteer for usability testing and other feedback methods like teachers, lawyers or paralegals, nurses, etc.

+ **Pound the (internet) pavement.** While you can head to college campuses or your local Starbucks to find a general audience, it'll save you time if you take your efforts to the web. Sites like Craigslist are always sure to bring in a large response, and social media sites are a good way to get the word out swiftly as well. If you're using social media, including a "please RT/repost" note has been proven to get your message to a wider audience. You can even go so far as to promote a tweet or buy a Facebook ad to reach more people, although you'll need to be careful about getting lost in the noise of ads. Because Facebook is heavily used for advertising, Facebooks users can become inoculated to ads and scroll right past yours. To combat this, work with a Facebook ad expert as possible.

In all cases, balance getting as close as you can to your target audience with your time and budget constraints, and always take participants' feedback with several grains of salt.

To build your test, you'll need to make a list of the relevant tasks performed by the target audience. Often this list will consist of the most common tasks, but if you're testing a new feature or a specific workflow, your task list should reflect that focus.

Here's an example list of common tasks for a project management tool:

+ Schedule meetings
+ Track milestones
+ Send updates
+ Store documents

+ Review deliverables
+ Track goals
+ Provide and manage feedback

This list includes general tasks. However, if you were working with a narrower focus, like developing a new feature for sharing documents and sending team communications, your list might look like this:

+ Add a new document to the project and tag individuals to review

+ Send an uploaded document to the internal team

+ Send a reminder about feedback due

+ Send a progress update to the team

The tasks get more specific as you focus on an individual feature or smaller project. Depending on your goal, your tasks might be more general (e.g., with a goal like "identify the main struggle with our most common workflows," your task might be "walk me through your morning routine in our app".) or more specific (e.g., with a goal like "increase usage of the calendar section among our most active users," a task might be "schedule a meeting with an attachment and multiple attendees".).

Once you've finalized your task list, prioritize your tasks in order of importance, first according to your project and testing goals and then by your target persona. The top 3 – 5 tasks in your prioritized list will be the basis of your scenarios. *Scenarios* are brief contextual stories that surround tasks. It's important to turn tasks into scenarios because scenarios are stories, and people connect to stories.

When you present someone with a list of tasks, they try to get the list done. By using a scenario, the context becomes as important as the task itself; it's a shortcut to getting your participants to empathize with the mindset relevant to the task being completed. Otherwise participants are likely to focus on completing the task rather than navigating the product as they normally would.

To create a scenario, go back to your research and personas: What context is most common for your personas when doing this task? What are the relevant details they would need? Which details are irrelevant? The latter question is extremely important, as you don't want to bog your scenarios down with needless information, which could be confusing or cause participants to get distracted. Let's look at an example.

PRO TIP

Goals Matter

Remember, in real life, the usage of your product and the available tasks are a way for people to achieve their goals. No one uses your product for its own sake even on sites like Facebook or Twitter. For apps that are more browse-focused, users' goals are not to use the app, even though that may seem like the purpose. Instead, the users' goals are really about wanting to connect and communicate with people or gain news and information.

In the previous section, we created the following task:

> *Add a new document to the project and tag individuals to review.*

To turn this into a scenario, consider the additional context someone would need if they were actually trying to do this task. First, they need to know their role and why they need to get the document reviewed. They will also need to know the names of people they need to tag. And possibly, although the task doesn't specifically call for this, they'd need to know the timeframe in which all this needs to happen.

Here's a resulting scenario for our example task:

> *As usual, managing your various projects can be a time sink in terms of getting responses and feedback from other team members, especially Michael and Bonnie. You've been using Project Y's project management tool for tracking due dates and milestones on your Brainstorming project and you're ready to test out the tool's potential for collecting feedback. You're hoping this will be a nice change from sending multiple files and reminders via email. Upload NewIdea.doc to the project and add Michael, Bonnie, and Jamie as people who need to provide feedback.*

As you can see, the scenario presents context and relevant details that the task alone lacks. Consider how you might try to complete this scenario differently than you would have if you had just been given the task. That's the power of scenarios.

The nuances of creating really successful scenarios can take time to master, but as long as the knowledge is conveyed succinctly in a story fashion with minimal leading language as discussed in Chapter 3, you're good to go. The story element is particularly important because it helps a participant make a connection and treat the scenario as they would in real life. It's a tough balance to tell a story and make a connection without overwhelming people with too much information so be sure to iterate and test your scenarios for effectiveness.

Once you've composed your scenarios, make sure that the scenarios can be completed on whatever product you're testing, and that whoever is running the test knows how each scenario can be completed. Knowing the scenario's solution is crucial, as you don't want to send your participants running down endless rabbit holes or trying to do things that cannot be done.

Additionally, if there are any scenario-relevant requirements, such as login credentials or form data, include that information with your scenarios and print both the information and the scenarios out. Never ask the participant to use personal information or make up information on the fly; that's not the purpose of the test and it's likely to make the participant uncomfortable.

Before finalizing your scenarios, ask a few team members to review them, in the context of your testing plan. You can even have them attempt to complete the scenarios to make sure they make sense and are possible. The extra eyes will help you be sure that you've covered things well, and that you haven't forgotten or misstated anything. Be sure to add your scenarios to your testing plan once they're finalized so that everyone is on the same page. And include any information needed for a given scenario on the same sheet as the scenario itself.

Facilitation and Observation

To run a usability test, you need a *facilitator*, and preferably 1 or 2 *observers*. As you might expect, a facilitator runs the test; this person interacts with the participant and keeps the test on track. Observers spend their time observing the test, making notes about instances where the participant becomes frustrated or confused, or does something unexpected.

Logistically speaking, facilitation is fairly straightforward. As a facilitator you will:

+ Print out scenarios, one per page, before each test. (You can reuse printed scenarios if they have not been marred in any way.)

+ Read the introductory script to the participant. (A script template can be found in the workbook.)

+ Ask any opener or ice-breaker questions to build rapport and help the participant feel comfortable.

+ Read one scenario at a time, and then hand the scenario and any relevant information to the participant, for their reference, asking the participant to think aloud through each task.

+ Transition the participant to each subsequent scenario.

+ End the test session by encouraging the participant to share any additional thoughts, feelings, or feedback.

+ Thank the participant for their time and give them details on how they will receive their incentive.

This all seems easy but facilitation is about more than simply executing these tasks. The main role that the facilitator plays during a usability test is not to run the test. It's actually to make the participant feel comfortable. Maximizing the gathered information and running the test are secondary to making the participant feel comfortable. So, what does that mean exactly?

Making the participant feel comfortable is about prioritizing the needs and experiences of a participant during a usability test. Because a usability test can often make a participant feel as if they are personally being tested, it's important to find ways to alleviate this feeling. By doing so, you'll help to maximize information you collect, because when people relax, they respond and react more naturally. This means that you not only get the maximum amount of information, but you'll also get more accurate information.

This is not to say that you cannot let a participant struggle to figure things out for a short time; indeed, this is exactly the type of thing you want to see, so you know where the real pain points are! But it's important to not let it go on too long, and to reassure participants that their struggle was actually helpful and not their fault.

The facilitator also has the opportunity to collect better and more information through occasionally prodding the participant and asking questions (sparingly!) throughout the test. Prodding, when the participant has stopped thinking aloud, or makes a "huh" noise. Asking questions, when the participant takes an action without explanation or makes a comment (like "this is odd") that needs clarification. Finding the balance of facilitation is challenging but after a few rounds of testing, you'll get the rhythm.

Another, less common but still valuable method of facilitation is the retrospective review. A *retrospective review* method of facilitation involves no thinking aloud, but instead asks participants to reflect on their experience once the test is complete. This is especially effective for participants who struggle to focus, or who have cognitive impairments, as interrupting their concentration can result in errors they wouldn't have otherwise made. It is also better for certain types of products, particularly those that have a lot of reading of content that require concentration. To read more about this method of facilitation, check out *The Handbook of Usability Testing* by Jeffrey Rubin and Dana Chisnell.

For observers, things are simpler: Observers literally observe the participant's actions during each test. However, it pays to practice and hone your observation skills, so you can note the helpful things while leaving the rest behind, as a usability test can move quickly and it won't be possible to capture everything. When capturing your observations, try to limit them to one observation per line on a spreadsheet or sticky note; this makes sorting and analyzing easier.

Observing works best when the participant and facilitator are in one room, and observers are in a separate room watching via a screen share or a two-way mirror. This keeps the participant from becoming intimidated by many people in the room, and it gives observers a free space to discuss the test as it's happening (if necessary), without interrupting the test.

There are many options for screensharing but you'll want to choose one that works for your situation. Here are a few we have used in our own tests:

Google Hangouts

Free, good for larger groups, each person joining must have an account, can have connectivity and audio issues, screen share can lag.

Skype

Free for 2 people, both people must have an account, hard to do group calls unless you have a paid account, can have connectivity issues

Join.me

Free for up to 3 people on the call, doesn't require login or download, no recording capabilities at free level

GoToMeeting

No free plan, most robust feature set and dial-in options, no recording capabilities at least expensive level

Zoom

Free for up to 100 participants, easy to use, no recording capabilities on the free plan, currently very popular

All of these options can work for both in-person and remote testing, although you'll want to research which one works best for your team's needs. Whatever software you choose, be sure to do at least one trial run of it before any actually tests, so you can work out any kinks in the process or identify extra steps that you'll want to share with your participant. Update your plan with how to adjust your testing process, based on any hiccups or challenges you discovered during the test run.

The final pieces you need for a comprehensive usability testing plan are a testing script and some conversational questions. We've included a template script and some questions in the workbook but you can modify them as needed. Before starting the test, read the test script out loud, and open with a few conversational ice-breaker questions. We also recommend ending the interactive portion of the test with a few follow-up questions to give closure on the test before moving on to any other activities. Once the main test is complete, it's common to conduct a more in-depth interview (about 10 – 15 minutes). Be sure to also prepare those questions in advance, following the guidelines about customer interviews described in Chapter 3. As with everything else, the script and questions should be included in the test plan.

Testing Day

On testing day, it's important to go in prepared. Here's a checklist we use to ensure that each test goes smoothly. We recommend adding to the checklist as needed:

+ Set up the testing room (whether physical or virtual).

+ Have the required software, websites, and applications loaded and ready to test on the appropriate machine, with all other systems and windows turned off.

+ Ensure that your scenarios are printed (one per page) and ready to provide to participants. In the case of remote testing, make sure the scenarios are easy to copy/paste into the meeting software chat window.

+ Confirm that your observers have all of the information they need in order to join the session.

+ Verify that your incentives are ready to go.

+ Confirm the appointment with each participant.

+ For remote participants,

- Be prepared to copy and paste each scenario into the chat window of your meeting software, so the participant can reference it after you've read it aloud.

- Make sure that anyone who joins is automatically muted, so there isn't a mid-test disruption. It's unsettling and can be embarrassing if someone loudly joins partway through the test (this has happened to Heather before, and it is not a good time).

Then you'll conduct the test:

1. Read the script.

2. Ask the ice-breaker questions. You don't have to stick strictly to these; the idea is just to get conversation flowing and get the participant feeling relaxed.

3. Open the appropriate site or document for testing, or direct the participant to do so on their own screen. Have them give you a brief description of what they see and what they think is happening on the page.

4. Read the first task. Then either hand the printout of the task to the participant, or paste it into the chat window so they can reference it. Watch as they start performing the task. Reminder: Reassure them if they seem worried or nervous about "messing up;" remind them to think out loud; ask them to clarify half-formed statements; and prevent them from struggling with a task for too long. (Observers: Take notes!)

5. Repeat Step 4 for each additional task.

6. Close out the test with some conversational or follow up questions, to help give the participant some closure about the test. (Note: Do not take these answers to heart; they are purely for the participant's sense of closure. If you want more information from the participant, plan to do a separate interview after the test.)

7. Conduct any additional interviews, card sorts, etc.

8. Thank them, specify how they will receive their incentive, and walk them out or log off.

Summary

Know if your decisions are the right ones by usability testing them with real or potential users. Usability testing allows you and your team to observe people who represent your target audience as they perform predefined tasks in your product. The test results can help you understand which parts of your product need additional work or refactoring.

Recruiting the right test subjects can be challenging. Employ smart strategies to find and entice great, persona-relevant test subjects. To get the most out of your usability tests, clarify your goals and develop a plan before you start testing. Take the time to design focused, relevant scenarios that will give you the results you need. Facilitate test sessions according to your plan, but also look for unexpected opportunities to gather additional information..

Put It in Action

Usability testing is an essential and powerful way to understand if your product or your designs make sense to your audience, in context. Using the workbook study template, fill in the the purpose, tasks, scenarios and communications for your usability test, as well as the personas you are targeting. Be sure to define the compensation you will offer participants and the methods you'll use for recruiting. Include a schedule as possible, and invite as many stakeholders and team members to the tests as possible.

Share the feedback tracking spreadsheet with your team members, so they can record their observations. Be sure all feedback is compiled and prepared for your analysis. We recommend using the KJ method outlined in Chapter 11 to analyze feedback with your team.

Measure Your Impact

CHAPTER TEN

Usability testing is all about qualitative data collection – getting feedback on why something isn't working and where systems break down.

Equally important to track is quantitative data, commonly called analytics. *Analytics* are metrics that can be counted and tracked over time using software – essentially the hard numbers behind how a product is being used. You can track many different analytics: bounce rate, time on page, number of clicks, amount of sales, and more.

Why Analytics?

It's nice to know the numbers, but what does tracking analytics actually get you? There are a few key reasons to track analytics, whether your product is brand new or has been in the market for years.

Establish Baselines

The first reason to track analytics is to establish baselines. *Baselines* are numbers that represent what's happening in your company now; this constitutes the starting point for all of your future measurement efforts. Essentially, they're the "you are here" marker of your organization. Without tracking the baseline of where you are now, you'll never know how close you are to those business goals you've set, or know when you've met those goals and can set new ones. For example, if your goal is to increase sign-ups by 10%, you need to know how many sign-ups you're getting now (your baseline), and you need a way to track that number over time: Are you getting closer to or farther from your goal?

Focus on the Right Things

Analytics also help you know where to focus your time. It can be overwhelming to figure out what to do next in moving your product forward. With good analytics, you can make smart decisions about your future activities. Two ways analytics help you focus are choosing projects and activities related to your goals and helping you identify sections of your product that have highest usage.

When it comes to your goals, consider what areas of your product would influence the outcome of your goals – then track and analyze usage and interactions on those areas. Coming back to our example goal of increasing sign-ups, by viewing the flow for your sign-up process (the sequence users have to go through to successfully sign up), you can see if there's one place where a large number of people are dropping off before completing, or if very few people even start the process. This way you don't spend time trying to improve a part of your product that will give marginal returns instead of solving the main problem. Once you've identified where a problem is happening, you can usability test that flow to find out exactly what the problem is and why it's causing users to struggle, so you can solve it successfully.

The sections of your product that get the highest usage are worth paying attention to if for no other reason than the most people see them. That means you have the greatest opportunity to create change that affects your business – from your goals to your tactics and strategies. It also gives you insight into what's important for your users. You can use that information to help you establish primary tasks for usability testing, new feature ideas and more.

Find Patterns

Patterns are important for understanding the details of your organization. Analytic tracking allows you to see the patterns that create long-term impact and success for your brand. This tracking also allows you to make smart decisions to maximize traffic, increase visibility with your target personas, and closemore sales. For example, do your blog posts get more traffic when you post them on Thursday mornings or Monday afternoons? Look at the patterns in your analytics and you'll know. Do you get more sales on weekends or on Wednesday evenings? Do people come to your site more in July or in December? Finding and analyzing patterns can help you grow your company over time.

Be careful about associating correlation with causation. Even though two independent variables seem to be related or caused by each other, they may not be. For example, let's say that your analytics tell you that engagement on your blog posts (comments, likes, or shares) has risen by 25% over the past 3 months. And in that same timeframe, your position in Google search results for a certain term has jumped from #7 to #2. It's tempting to conclude that the increased engagement around your content has made your site more credible in Google's eyes, and boosted your rank. (And if that turns out to be true, great! Give your writers and content marketers a bonus.)

However, it could actually be something else entirely: Maybe a third independent factor has boosted your PageRank score (Google may even have tweaked the algorithm in a way that favors you), and your higher rank has allowed more people to find your site and engage with your posts. Try to look across more of your analytics to get a fuller picture of the causes and effects at work.

What Should You Track?

When it comes to analytics tracking, there's an overwhelming amount of both data and tracking software out there, making it hard to know where to start or what to track. Before choosing your software, you'll want to consider what you actually want to track; this way you can choose software that works best for your needs (or alternatively, create your own internal tracking system). The easiest way to figure out what data you need is to focus exclusively on the goals you've created, working from the business goals down; your goals will give you clear information about what to track.

How do goals help? Let's take an example: If your goal is to get more sign-ups, then track the number of sign-ups, as well as everything related to signing up, including all parts of the sign-up process: things like the most commonly visited pages that lead to someone signing up, and how many people who sign up are actually in your target audience or primary personas. Whatever your goals are, there are actions, workflows, and data points that you can track to better understand what is happening now and how your analytics change as you make updates.

It's a good rule of thumb to always track any activity on your site that makes you money. The most obvious money-making task is any product or service you sell that someone can buy right on your site. So at the very least you'll want to track analytics related to the checkout process, especially metrics like the percentage of people who fail to finish the checkout process at each step of your checkout flow and abandoned cart rates; these metrics are crucial to your business.

But there are other money-related actions you can track as well. Do you use banner ads? You'll want to track how effective they are – including number of interactions, load-time issues, and more. If you sell products or services that require people to get in touch with you before purchasing, track the process by which they contact you: Are you seeing a lot of unfinished or abandoned forms?

If you have an app with existing users, you can still track monetary opportunities with those users. Are there features that require an upgrade? How many people try to use those features without the upgrade? Are the users converting? If not, what are they doing instead? Any action someone takes that could lead to money for you is a must-track item.

You'll also want to track feedback information, which can come from:

+ social media messages,

+ logs about the frequency of error messages in your product

+ customer service or help desk questions

+ feature requests,

+ and other similar sources.

This type of data is valuable because it provides you with a direct line into the concerns, struggles, and frustrations that your users have, at scale. By monitoring feedback, you can enable yourself and your team to make smarter decisions about where to spend time researching, testing, and updating.

Tracking Analytics

Now that you have a good sense of what to track, it's time to figure out how to track it. We've covered some of the most common methods and tools here, but it's important to find the ones that work best for you.

Google Analytics

The mother of all analytics software, Google Analytics works for almost every organization no matter the size, industry, or purpose. There are two main reasons everyone uses Google Analytics:

+ It's free

+ Google has access to data across the majority of the internet

Those are really good reasons to use Google Analytics. If you use nothing else, set up your organization with a Google Analytics account. Even if you don't have time to view it now, tracking starts as soon as you set it up, so when you're ready, your data will be there.

Setting up Google Analytics is pretty easy at the basic level. You sign up for a Google Analytics account, and then you add a tracking code to your product's HTML. If you want to track specific goals or events, there are some additional steps you need to follow; check the Google Analytics website for the latest instructions. Events can include clicks, form field typing, form completion, purchases, and more.

Once you've set up Google Analytics, it can be intimidating to figure out where to go to get useful information. Here are 3 reports we recommend as a starting point:

USERS FLOW

This report is located in the Audience section of the Google Analytics reports and it's possibly the most valuable non-event-based report available. It's exactly what it says: users' flows. This report shows you the path that people take to and from each page on your site. This is a perfect report for understanding where people are going in your product, where they drop off, and how they arrive. The great thing is that you can select any page or you can follow any audience segment to see their specific flows.

MOBILE OVERVIEW

This report is also located in the Audience section, in the mobile overview. The most important part of this report isn't the graph; it's actually the table below the graph, which shows you the breakdown of which devices people are on when they visit your product. This is especially helpful if you're considering something like creating a native mobile app; this report will tell you if enough people are using mobile to make it worthwhile.

EVENTS

Located in the Behaviors section, the entire Events subsection is a wealth of valuable information about the events you've set up for your product. You can use this area to understand the results of your events: Are people starting to fill out your contact form but not hitting Send? Do people forget to save their notification preferences? If you've set up an event, this is where you can track and view it.

Google Analytics can seem overwhelming, but it contains a wealth of useful data if you know where to look. Start small and build up your understanding of what other data and reports give you useful information as you have time. It's better to stay focused on useful data rather than trying to capture and interpret any data you can find.

This method of data collection is fairly popular at this point, so it's likely you've heard of it or even run your own tests. An *A/B test* or *split test* is a test in which you create two or more variations of a product, most commonly website or sales page designs. The multiple versions are then randomly displayed to people who use the product, and results are tracked on which version "performed better." To successfully run an A/B test, you need a few key things:

+ **Multiple variations of the product being tested.** These can be as simple as a button color or heading change or as dramatic as two completely different products.

+ **A measure of success.** This is what you will use to determine which variation performed better. For webpages, it's usually related to sign-ups or purchases; with applications, it's usually related to usage, retention, or customer service or help requests.

+ **Software or a method for serving variations randomly.** You can't test multiple versions without actually getting eyes on each version. You can accomplish this manually, by creating multiple ads that drive traffic to a different URL for each version, or you can get your development team to set up some code that delivers different versions. Alternatively, you can use a service that allows you to create variations for testing and automatically serves up different versions.

Be sure to carefully consider the impact to your users when you run A/B tests, especially when A/B testing an app or parts of an app. We learned this the hard way in January of 2015: We had just decided to sign Jen's J-term course students up for free trials of a UX project management tool as part of the course and reached out to the software team to finalize everything. Two days after all of the students had been set up, the company launched an A/B test on their entire product, and included Jen's class in the test. Suddenly Jen was trying to troubleshoot problems for software she couldn't even see for half of her class. Needless to say, she did not use that software for subsequent courses.

Customer Service

Customer service reps (CSRs) are an organization's most underutilized and valuable source of data. They have a direct line to the concerns, frustrations, and needs of your customers at scale. The trick is to implement a system to capture that data.

If you're lucky, your CSRs are using a customer relationship management (CRM) solution like Salesforce or Zendesk, through which you can automate your tracking processes, at least partially. If you're using one of these systems, set up specific tags or labels to classify feedback based on features, behaviors, or functionality. Then ask your CSRs to apply the tags to each conversation they have; this will help you view all the feedback of one type simultaneously so you can look for common patterns.

If your company isn't using a CRM, you can implement a manual method that does the same thing. Instead of tags in a software tool, create a spreadsheet with one tag per column, and ask your CSRs to tally the number of conversations they have about each tag topic. It won't be as detailed as the CRM method (unless your CSRs are willing to add a lot of information to the spreadsheet), but it will still give you insight into the areas of biggest concern for your customers and visitors.

Internal Logging System

If you're at a company that has an existing product out in the world, it's likely that you have access to another group of people who are already thinking about analytics (on some level): systems engineers. Anybody who manages servers or databases is probably already using a logging system to record certain events at the server level that might indicate trouble: things like failed login attempts, or database requests coming from outside your company's environment.

These might not sound exactly like the events you most want to track, but they can still be a source of valuable information that can influence design. Start a conversation with your engineers. Ask them what types of events they track in their logging system, and how and when they typically review that information. You may be surprised by how much you can learn from the tools they're already using. If you build up enough goodwill, you can even ask them to track specific elements that support the work you're doing. And if you're starting with a new product, you can make your tracking needs part of the product requirements as it is built.

Summary

Much has been written about qualitative vs. quantitative data collection – but the question "which is better?" obscures the fact that a healthy product development process needs both. Analytics can tell you the what, but usually not the why; usability testing gets you into the mind of your users, but won't help you measure your success against the hard numbers that define and shape your business.

Use analytics help you establish baselines, focus on doing high-value work, and identify usage patterns. To start, collect, analyze, and respond to quantifiable metrics that indicate how your product is being used. When deciding what to track, refer to your organizational strategy and goals. Also track any activity that makes you money. Don't try to track every possible data point for completion's sake. In addition to deploying a dedicated analytics tool like Google Analytics, consider any insights that you can glean through A/B split testing, your CSR, or your internal logging system.

The lesson about analytics is: start right now. The sooner you begin to build your baseline and understand how things are today, the better you'll be able to track your progress toward your goals. And above all, remember that numbers are just numbers; they only have the meaning that we give them.

Put It in Action

Metrics help you understand the way people use your product at scale. If you take nothing else from this chapter, be sure to set up Google Analytics now. It will start tracking immediately, so you'll have the data when you're ready to use it.

Once you're ready to review your metrics, use the workbook to help you identify which metrics you want to track, reviewing your goals, your audiences' goals and other relevant information. For each metric, note any methods you can use to get that data, and decide on the best way to do so. You can also use the A/B testing worksheet to set up and run A/B tests on different parts of your product, identify the variables you are testing, and the timeframe and process for each.

Finally, be sure to develop relationships with other teams in your company; customer service teams, data analysts and systems engineers can help you gather more data about your product, as you have more questions and continue iterating.

IDEA VALIDATION

DESIGN VALIDATION

PLANNING

Your Results

Analyze

Between customer interviews, usability testing, A/B testing, and Google Analytics tracking, you and your team now have piles of notes, observations, metrics, and numbers all waiting to be assigned meaning or discarded into the void.

Having come this far, it's hard to believe there's still more to do. But you have to make sense of all that data. How do you do that?

Two Types of Data

When you do any kind of research, testing, or tracking, you generate at least one of two types of data: quantitative and qualitative.

Quantitative Data

Quantitative data is data that can be measured and represented in numbers; it's information about quantities. Number of visitors, dollar value of a sale, percentage of people on mobile, time spent on a task: These are all examples of quantitative data. Quantitative data can be graphed or displayed in a spreadsheet. Basically, quantitative data tells us what has happened (e.g., 10 people downloaded the mobile app).

PRO TIP

Be Careful:

Even though it's numerically based, quantitative data isn't actually more or less objective. Because data is meaningless until we assign it value or meaning, the data we use is only as objective as we are (and no one is truly objective).

Qualitative Data

Qualitative data is data about qualities, or things that cannot be measured in numbers. The relative softness of a kitten is a good example of qualitative data. In your work, qualitative data might include workflows, feedback, frustrations people experience while using the product, how usable a product is, and more. In all of these examples, you cannot assign a number to any of those items; they can't be measured exactly. You can track patterns in qualitative data, such as the frequency with which a particular qualitative data point comes up, but the end data is still qualitative. That doesn't mean it's less important; in fact, it can be more important, since qualitative data can tell us why something happened. Understanding why is crucial in solving a problem correctly.

Don't Inadvertently Jump to Conclusions Based on Quantitative Data Alone.

For example, 70% of people visiting your website may have abandoned their shopping cart, but this number doesn't tell you why that happened. You may have some ideas, but this is speculation without further research. Your next step should be to create and run a usability test so you can pinpoint the reasons for abandonment in the flow. This generates qualitative data that helps clarify the meaning of the quantitative data you already have.

Understanding the types of data you have can also help you ask better questions in your work, particularly around any tracking and testing you are doing. You'll be able to tailor your research and really focus in on the most challenging problems faced by your users.

As you may have guessed, these two types of data work best when they work together. Knowing how to analyze and make sense of each is important, so you can draw real conclusions.

Analyzing Quantitative Data

Analyzing quantitative data is important because until you ascribe meaning, all of the data is just numbers. Five percent open rate on your emails? That might be higher than normal and really great. Or it might be so low that you delete the email and all history of its existence. As in everything, context matters. And to understand the context of the data you've collected, you need to come back to your organization's goals, as well as your mission and vision. Since these are the things your organization is striving for, it makes sense to interpret your data through that lens.

A website like Facebook wants its users to log in frequently; indeed, one of its key success metrics is daily active users (DAU). But for an electric company, a high number of DAUs visiting the company website in between billing cycles could indicate an outage in an area, or some other change or concern. Since most people log in to their account only to pay their bill (if at all, since auto-pay is common), a large number of people logging in before the month's bill has been sent out is actually unlikely to be a good thing. Context matters.

Sit down with your data handy and review your organization's goals, mission, and vision. Ask yourself some version of the following questions, to add context to what you've collected, layer by layer:

+ What does your data you've collected tell you about how close you are to achieving your goals?

+ If you've been around for a while, how does this month's data compare to where you were at this time last month? Last year?

+ Look for patterns. Are your numbers trending one way or another?

+ Are there random fluctuations that give you pause? Does the data make sense with everything else you know about your business?

Asking all of these questions and more is how you figure out what the data means and how you decide what to test to understand why these numbers are happening.

PRO TIP

Identify Outliers with Caution

You're likely to notice some outliers in your data. Outliers are data points that don't seem to fit the normal pattern that you can see for a given metric. Outliers are sometimes excluded from analysis, since they don't speak to the primary trend or pattern. Use care in excluding data though; what may seem like an outlier in your analytics system may actually be a warning sign for future problems your users might have.

Analyzing Qualitative Data with the KJ Method

Qualitative data can be trickier to analyze than quantitative data since every user is unique, with different views of the world. Since each user is different, many of your observations will be different, even if you run the same test every time. However, by analyzing qualitative data and making sense of all of those observations, you'll have the best information to indicate the right actions that will improve your product.

Frequently at the end of usability testing, someone (you? a stakeholder?) becomes obsessed with one specific piece of feedback that came up during testing. For that person, the problem is huge, hairy, and OMG MY HAIR IS ON FIRE FIX THIS PROBLEM NOW. To them, other problems seem much less important and it can be hard to determine if they are right or just fixated. How do you decide?

You can prioritize by sexiness, the perceived urgency of HAIR ON FIRE, and what's "easiest," or you can prioritize based on what's truly necessary. To define what's actually necessary, you'll want to review your goals and work with your team. This means we need to base our analysis on the data patterns we found for problem areas in our product, and from everyone on the team, not just the CEO or the dude with the big mouth that dominates every meeting with his agenda.

Generally speaking, there are two types of approaches to analyzing qualitative data:

+ You, as the research leader, take the observations, complete your own analysis, and write a (often lengthy) usability report. You read all of the observations and, using your opinions, biases, and experience with technology, you determine what they mean. You make recommendations for what should be fixed or changed.

  - **Advantage:** No pesky opinions or arguments to deal with! Your decisions rule the day!

  - **Disadvantage:** Did you really get the right answer and interpret all of the information correctly? Will anyone read the report? Is anyone invested in the recommendations you made and willing to take action?

- Involve the team in the data analysis. Generate some kind of group discussion, where everyone can talk about the outcome and their observations, and together you can prioritize what things should be fixed.

  - **Advantage:** No usability report to write! Everyone works together to find the answer!

  - **Disadvantage:** What about that guy who dominates the whole meeting? Will anyone disagree with the CEO's opinion? What if someone has a change of heart later?

In general, involving your team in all levels of user testing is the best way to let the users' feedback positively influence your product. After all, the product was built for them. The fact that the CEO wants the button placed somewhere else should be immaterial, unless she is the sole user of the product. Unfortunately, you can't always escape this top-down design experience, but by involving your team and having a plan, you can circumvent design-by-opinion as much as possible.

Once you've decided on team analysis, how do you ensure that all observations and opinions are considered, when these discussions could be so politically charged?

The *KJ Method* helps get around all these problems, while still analyzing our qualitative data. Also called an *affinity diagram*, the KJ Method is designed to analyze, group, and prioritize qualitative observations, without one person dominating the discussion, while ensuring that all viewpoints are considered.

User Interface Engineering (UIE) , a UX agency, wrote a comprehensive article on the KJ Method. Using the steps that they've outlined, we'll provide our variation on this valuable method for qualitative observation analysis.

Step 0: Choose a Facilitator

Before you begin, assign someone on your team to facilitate the process. This person will be responsible for keeping everyone on track, managing each step of the process, and ensuring people remain silent during the various activities. They will also collect and send out the results of the analysis, so everyone has it for reference when moving forward.

You'll need a pile of blank sticky notes of any size or color.

You'll need pens for writing. Preferably, use a dark pen that can be read from a few feet away.

You'll need a stretch of blank wall. Test to make sure that the sticky notes will stick to the wall. Alternatively, use a large conference room table; in this case, you can use index cards instead of sticky notes, if you prefer. For both options,, it's easy to take a photo of the in-progress and final results, so you don't have to transfer and reassemble it later.

Jen likes to use a roll of plain brown paper on a conference table in combination with sticky notes. When the team has completed their analysis, the results can be rolled up and transported anywhere. (Why brown paper? It's pretty cheap, and it comes in big rolls, so you have plenty of room for the analysis.)

Step 2: Determine a Focus Question

In general, this question will be, "What did we learn from our usability testing?" In this case, you'll examine all of the observations that you gathered during your user testing. However, if your team is focusing on one area of the usability test, you could use a question like, "Why were users unable to fill out the form?" In that case, your observations will focus on the specific test feedback that's relevant to the form , even if you have other feedback.

Step 3: Organize the Group

Who is involved with the data analysis? Ideally, it's everyone who was involved with user testing, except the users themselves. This includes the facilitator and the observers, as well as anyone on the product team; everyone might not be able to make it, but ensure that most parts of the product team are represented in some form. If the group grows large, break into smaller groups during the analysis, and then summarize across groups at the end.

To prepare everyone, send out the test observations in advance of the meeting; while everyone may not review it (stakeholders, we're looking at you), sending the observations beforehand gives your team members the opportunity to gather their thoughts before they come to the meeting. This way, there will be less likelihood of changes of heart after the meeting's results are decided.

Step 4: Put Opinions (or Data) onto Sticky Notes

Transcribe each observation for each user onto its own sticky note. You can ask your observers to each do their own or you can take the full list and do it yourself. (If you're doing it yourself, do it before the meeting, so everyone is not just watching you write.) There will be some duplication; that's OK. The visual of a stack of sticky notes that say similar things is valuable when analyzing the data in later steps. (Be sure to recycle the used sticky notes when you're done!)

Ask that your observers write legibly and large enough to read the note from a few feet away.

No one should talk during this step! Transcribe in silence.

Step 5: Put Sticky Notes on the Wall

Place all of the sticky notes on the table or the wall, so none is blocked by another note. The notes don't need to be in any particular order, but they should all be legible at a distance of a few feet.

No one should talk during this step! Resist the urge to arrange the sticky notes into patterns.

Step 6: Group Similar Items

The first rule in grouping similar items is that there is no talking among meeting attendees!!! (Yes, really. No talking! The facilitator is the only person talking throughout the next few steps.)

Ask everyone in the meeting to group notes that they see as being similar to each other. For example, "user can't find Contact button" and "user can't find About page" might be grouped together, as these are both navigation problems.

There are no rules for what can be grouped together and no size restrictions either. A single note can be its own group if that's warranted.

Keep in mind that just because one person puts some sticky notes into a group doesn't mean that group is final. Another person may rearrange that group, moving items in or out of it, breaking it into multiple groups or even adding it wholesale to another group. If there is some disagreement that persists – members take the same note or notes and put them in different groups over and over again – simply make another copy of the note so a copy can be put in each location.

This process continues until everyone is satisfied with the arrangement of notes (just ask them to sit when they are done).

Remember, no talking.

Step 7: Name Each Group

There is still no talking for attendees!

Once the groups are created, ask participants to name each group. Group names can be new, written on a sticky note and stuck above the group, or they can be one of the observations that are already a part of the group. As with the last step, tell participants to sit when they are satisfied with the group names.

During this process, participants may find that some groups should actually be split into other groups, or groups should be lumped into one. It's fine to continue rearranging the groups as needed during this process.

By the end of this step, each group will have a name so it's easy to reference later. An added benefit at this point is that everyone will have read every sticky note on the wall, even if they didn't read them in advance, and will have a sense of which ones they think are important.

There's no talking for attendees for this step too.

Read the focus question set in step one out loud to the meeting attendees one more time. Remind everyone that this is the important question to answer in the analysis, and that the sticky-note groups should focus on answers to that question. That means when voting, you want attendees to prioritize groups of feedback that are aligned with answering the question. Basically if the feedback group doesn't relate to answering the focus question, then you won't want to vote for that group. In the most basic scenario of "what did we learn," everyone should vote for the groups that represent the most important things learned from usability testing.

Each participant gets a total of six votes, which can be represented by small stickers or by check marks made with a Sharpie. For example, participants may distribute those votes across their top three groups, with 3 votes to the most crucial, 2 votes to the next most crucial and 1 vote to the next after that. However, there's no rule to how anyone distributes their votes, so someone could place all their votes on one group, if they felt strongly.

Everyone's opinion on what is important has equal weight at this stage and all opinions are "heard."

Notice that, in this step, we've cleverly turned our qualitative data into quantitative data

No talking. This is very important!

PRO TIP

The Secret of No Talking

Most of this process involves not speaking, with good reason. At some point, you've been in a meeting in which one person completely dominates the conversation, often to the detriment of the process. When people have to fight to get a word in edgewise, certain voices are never heard and that one dominant person's ideas are overrepresented in that meeting, whether they are good or not.

By not allowing any talking, you level the playing field of communication; it's almost impossible to be overbearing in your opinions if you cannot do more than move a sticky note or place a check mark on a group. Everyone's voice is given equal weight and the results reflect a shared solution.

Now, you can talk.

As the meeting facilitator, you must tally up the votes and read them off for each group. The top three groups represent the most important items to address in this round of product updates, and you can work with your team on building your backlog accordingly.

What Happens Next?

Now you've analyzed and prioritized your data. You've identified your next round of problems to fix. Where do you go next? Well, that depends on your problems.

User testing can turn up problems and issues in just about every area of the product lifecycle:

+ Wrong goals for the product or user

+ Wrong target audience

+ Wrong personas

+ Poor branding

+ Jumbled information architecture (IA)

+ Poor user interface (UI) or user experience (UX)

Most people assume that a majority of problems are caused by a bad user interface. However, the user interface is only as good as your goals, target audience, personas, branding, and IA. If one observation was that a user couldn't find a button where they expected it to be, the surface-level solution is to assume that the interface needs to change; digging deeper, you may find that the content leading to that point was confusing, or that the IA doesn't actually support your target audience's goals. These underlying issues still may result in changes to the interface, but the changes will be more impactful because the solutions were created from a complete understanding of the problem, rather than a surface-level understanding.

At this point, you'll want to create a backlog or plan for tackling each of the problems in your top 3 groups and use that plan to assign different projects and tasks to your team. For some problems, you may need to take several steps back in your organization to really fix the root of the problem; if you don't have time or budget, you may simply create a quick fix that solves the immediate need. In either case, update your wireframes and, if you have time, test again to ensure that you're on the right track with your changes.

Summary

Once you've done both quantitative and qualitative data tracking and collection, analyze data in the context of your organizational goals, mission, and vision. While analyzing data, identify patterns and search for any subtleties that might lie beneath the surface. One common and successful for analyzing data is the KJ Method, which allows people to all have a say without spending hours in opinion wars. After analyzing, use the results of your analysis to form the basis of a task list or development backlog.

Put It in Action

Analyzing both qualitative and quantitative data is essential to moving forward. In the workbook you'll find a template for analyzing your quantitative findings, as well as a results sheet for your qualitative analysis using the KJ method. Use these templates to share your findings and results in a readable format.

The workbook also includes templates to help you keep track of your analyses over time, so you can review your data for patterns and see your business and product change over time. You'll also be able to track your progress on various goals.

NOW May I Code?

Once you've addressed the core problems identified from testing and finalized your wireframes, you're ready to build your product in code.

While it's tempting to start coding without doing the activities outlined in this book, we caution against doing that. By defining your business, product and user goals, articulating your brand and message, and doing the work to design and test your product at low fidelity, you're much more likely to create something that succeeds upon launch.

And we would know. We've both worked with clients to do this work for their products, resulting in a 25% increase in sales over a quarter, a 5-star app launch, $100,000 in grant funding based on a well-defined and tested prototype and more. The reason these steps are so effective is that they save time and create focus. Remember the following themes we've covered about the value of advance planning:

+ Planning your projects and aligning them to the needs of both your business and your target audiences keeps you focused on the end goals you want to achieve. Having an articulate plan with specific goals can help you end opinion wars, stop scope creep, and make smarter decisions, ultimately helping you create a better product.

+ It's MUCH easier to change your idea in the early stages, when it's a low fidelity design or still just a back-of-the-napkin concept, than it is to make the same change in code later. User and competitor research, sketching, wireframing, and usability testing are all designed to help you model & evaluate different approaches and solutions quickly, with little wasted effort.

+ Early-stage plans, content, and designs invite better, more actionable critique. With unfinished and obviously in-progress work, not only will clients and stakeholders give more candid feedback, you'll be in a better place to make all the changes necessary to create the product your customers need. An hour of planning can save you months of potential headaches in after-the-fact changes.

In other words, don't rush to code! Enjoy this time while your website or application is in its strategy and planning stages. Understand how your product will fit within the market and who will benefit from it. Run a few rounds of testing and development to make sure your product is honed to the right audiences it before you code it. While it's relatively easy to move small user interface elements after you've coded and launched your product, if you've gotten your target audience, your site architecture, or your goals wrong, your product isn't going to be successful.

Your Mileage May Vary

Nothing works 100% of the time and not everything here may be the right fit for your team, your business or your product. That's cool with us. We encourage you to take what you need and leave behind whatever doesn't serve your efforts. And check back in from time to time – what isn't needed now may be just the thing to move you forward in a few months.

You Got This

We hope this book has inspired you to create your next website or application with intention, by establishing a clear vision, validating with an impartial perspective, and using an informed decision-making process. As we've demonstrated in these chapters, a little forethought and planning can go a long way to ensuring your product's success, time after time. And it can make all the difference for your product.

To your (planned) success!

Reading List

Books

Content Strategy for the Web,
Second Edition by Kristina Halvorson & Melissa Rach

Don't Make Me Think (3rd Edition) & Rocket Surgery Made Easy
by Steve Krug

Gamestorming by Dave Gray, Sunni Brown, James Macanufo

Mental Models & Practical Empathy by Indi Young

Making Sense of Any Mess by Abby Covert

The User's Journey by Donna Lichaw

Managing Chaos by Lisa Welchman

Why We Fail by Victor Lombardi

Liminal Thinking by Dave Gray

The Design of Everyday Things by Don Norman

Build Better Products by Laura Klein

Validating Product Ideas by Tomer Sharon

The Startup Equation by Ja-Naé Duane and Steve Fisher

Product Roadmaps Relaunched by C Todd Lombardo, Bruce McCarthy,
Evan Ryan, and Michael Connors

Radical Focus & Pencil Me In by Christina Wodtke

Handbook of Usability Testing by Jeffery Rubin and Dana Chisnell

Influencer by Brittany Hennessy

How to Transform Your Ideas into Software Products by Poornima
Vijayashanker

Start With Why by Simon Sinek

Grit by Angela Duckworth

Accessibility for Everyone by Laura Kalbag

Banish Your Inner Critic by Denise Jacobs

Mismatch by Kat Holmes

Badass: Making Users Awesome by Kathy Sierra

Atomic Design by Brad Frost

Websites, Magazines and Blogs

https://theuxnotebook.com/

https://inclusionatwork.co/

https://uxbooth.com/

https://www.contentstrategy.com/

https://stackingthebricks.com/

https://eleganthack.com/

https://www.smashingmagazine.com/articles/

https://articles.uie.com/

https://www.ideo.com/blog

http://boxesandarrows.com/

https://fromfoundertoceo.com/podcasts/

https://blog.pixelsforhumans.com

Glossary

5-second test: A method of user research where someone is shown a page, wireframe, or other digital artifact for 5 seconds, then asked to share their impressions and other information about the artifact.

a/b split test: A randomized experiment that tests the relative success of two or more variants of a website, landing page or application.

Accomplish mentality: a mental model where a user is focused on achieving or accomplishing a specific task or goal.

Affinity diagram/KJ method: Process for organizing a large number of ideas into groups and prioritizing the various groups. It was created in the 1960s by Japanese anthropologist Jiro Kawakita.

Analytics: The hard numbers or measurable data from your website or application.

Application (app): A computer program designed to run in a web browser or mobile device such as a phone/tablet or watch.

Assumptions: A thing that is accepted as true or as certain to happen without proof.

Attribute: A quality or feature regarded as a characteristic or inherent part of someone or something.

Baseline: The numbers that represent what's happening in your company now; this constitutes the starting point for all of your future measurement efforts.

Brand: A company name, logo, colors, message, and perceived and chosen attributes.

Brand style guide: A document that contains all brand rules and constraints, including, but not limited to: a list of approved colors with usage context; logo variations of different sizes, shapes, and colors, including usage style restrictions; approved fonts; and other design elements.

Browsing mentality: A mental model where someone using a site or application does not have a specific goal or take in mind.

Business goals: The highest level goals your company and product are trying to achieve.

Cart sort: A research method where in you as participants to organize words and phrases into different groups and label each group.

Client: A person or organization using the services of a professional person or company.

Code: The symbolic arrangement of data or instructions in a computer program or the set of such instructions.

Cognitive empathy: The intentional effort to understand the needs, perspectives, contexts and emotions of another person.

Common pattern: A pattern that's used frequently in your target audience's experience, often in their experience with the internet. The most basic example of this is a text link: blue and underlined.

Competitor analysis: A review of other companies and organizations in the same or similar industries as yours to understand how existing and potential customers view and interact with those orgs, and your competitor's strengths and weaknesses. Also a mechanism to develop effective competitive strategies in your target market.

Competitors: Other companies, organizations and businesses that are competing for the same things, whether customers, funding, or anything else.

Constraint: Limits that provide boundaries for projects, products, and requirements.

Content audit: The creation of a list of all your content, where it exists on your site, the URL of the content and what pages link to each piece of content.

Content creator: Person responsible for creating the content requested, and making updates to the content as needed, including incorporating feedback.

Content governance: The strategy for creating and managing your content over time.

Content owner: Person responsible for requesting content, receive feedback on it from various editors, keeping it up-to-date, and archiving it if needed.

Content strategy: The method by which you determine the content you need, and the process for creating, updating, and maintaining all of the content within your product or site over time.

Content structure: The process or details of how to create your content. The subcomponents of content structure provide the blueprints for crafting new content and updating current content in a consistent way so, like your brand, your content is always properly representing your organization.

Content type: A reusable collection of metadata for a category of content, with its corresponding taxonomies that allows you to manage information in a centralized, reusable way.

Content/editorial calendar: A schedule for creating, updating, and archiving content, for each type of content you need.

Core content strategy: The main mission statement for your content. It guides you in how to best create and repurpose the content in your product to help meet the organization's goals.

Core message: The single most important thing you want people to know after viewing your content. All of your content, from images and icons to text, should echo this message.

Customer interviews: Long, one-sided conversations with individuals who are part of your audience with the intention of understanding their perspective, mental models, needs, contexts and goals as they relate to your product.

Customer Service Reps (CSRs): The team members at an organization who interact directly with customers, to answer questions and troubleshoot problems. They have a direct line to the concerns, frustrations, and needs of your customers at scale.

Data: Facts and statistics collected together for reference or analysis.

Deliverable: A body of work you create and deliver, whether to yourself, to your company, or to your customers or clients.

Design system: A collection of reusable components, guided by clear standards, that can be assembled together to build any number of application.

Development: The process of coding.

Empathy Map: A technique (developed by Dave Gray) in which you ask meeting attendees (usually your team members and stakeholders) to empathize with and understand a specific audience by considering what they think, feel, see, say, do, and hear, as well as the pains they face and the benefits you can offer them.

External Risk: A risk coming from the outside: a bad economy, war, or stock market performance, for example.

Features: A distinctive attribute or aspect of something.

Flat design: A design style where elements are two-dimensional or "flat" in appearance,

Focus Audience: The intended audience or readership of a publication, advertisement, or other message.

Freelancer: A person who works for other companies on a contract basis.

Functionality: How a product works.

Google Analytics: A commonly used, basic analytics tracking program.

Grid-based layout: A page structure that is arranged and divided into equal rows and columns, making it easier to design web pages without having to use floats and positioning.

Ideal client: The perfect or target audience or persona for a product or service.

Information architecture: The way we arrange and organize information to make it understandable.

Interaction elements: Any elements in your interface that do something. This category spans the full breadth of interaction on the web and computers in general – from a basic link to another page, to a form that captures data, to a search query results page, to a full-featured game.

Internal Risk: A risk within the project: for example, loss of funding, reduction of resources, or a change in management.

Iterate: Consider other ways of saying the same thing, or other images or icons that might communicate the same ideas.

KJ method/Affinity diagram: Designed to analyze, group, and prioritize qualitative observations, without one person dominating the discussion, while ensuring that all viewpoints are considered. It was created in the 1960s by Japanese anthropologist Jiro Kawakita.

Landing page: A stand-alone web page focused on one message, one product and one action.

Logo: A symbol or other design adopted by an organization to identify its products, uniform, vehicles, etc.

Mental models: Conscious and unconscious expectations about how something should be or work based on past experiences.

Metrics: A method of measuring something, or the results obtained from this.

Milestone: A point in time when a key deliverable or a group of deliverables is complete.

Minimum viable product (MVP): A product with just enough features to satisfy early customers, and to provide feedback for future product development.

Mission statement: The overall purpose of a company.

Mobile-first: A design philosophy popularized by Luke Wroblewski that calls for web practitioners to design for small screens (and other typical mobile-device constraints) first.

Most advanced yet acceptable (MAYA): A product creation philosophy that states that advancements need to happen in incremental stages to be adopted broadly and successfully.

Open Source Software: Software that's distributed with its source code, making it editable by anyone with an interest in doing so.

Out of scope: Features, functionality, artifacts or deliverables that are not included in the current set of project work.

Outlier: A person or thing differing from all other members of a particular group or set.

Persona: Archetypes of users that are based on research from actual users. Also referred to as a target audience or ideal client, a persona becomes a representation of a group of users with the same (or closely related) goals, needs, behaviors, and contexts.

Pricing Structure: An approach in products and services pricing which defines various prices, discounts, offers consistent with the organization goals and strategy.

Process: A series of actions or steps taken in order to achieve a particular end.

Product: An article or substance that is manufactured or refined for sale. In this book, it refers to any website, or application.

Product goals: The purpose of your product. Why it exists and what it exists to do or achieve.

Project management: The practice of initiating, planning, executing, controlling, and closing the work of a team to achieve specific goals and meet specific success criteria at the specified time.

Project plan: The objective of a project plan is to define the approach to be used by the project team to deliver the intended project management scope of the project.

Project purpose: The reason a project needs to be done; what it needs to achieve to be considered successful or complete.

Proprietary software: Software that does not allow you to access the source code, meaning you cannot modify the software on an individual level through the code.

Proto-persona: Created from internal group consensus about who the audience is without any research.

Qualitative data: Data and feedback on a product. Not countable (i.e. the fluffiness of a kitten is qualitative).

Quantitative data: Numerical data.

Research: The systematic investigation into and study of materials and sources in order to establish facts and reach new conclusions.

Research Explanations: The definitions of different aspects of a research session you will need to share with a research participant.

Research facilitation: The process of running a research session.

Research goal: The purpose of a research project or sessions.

Research Incentive: A gift that is awarded to research participants once they have participated in research; often monetary in nature.

Research observation: An observed data point from a specific research session.

Research questions: The questions you ask as part of your research.

Retrospective review: A method of facilitation involves no thinking aloud, but instead asks participants to reflect on their experience once the test is complete.

Revenue Streams: A revenue stream is a source of money for a company or organization. In business, a revenue stream is generally made up of either recurring revenue, transaction-based revenue, project revenue, or service revenue. In government, the term revenue stream often refers to different types of taxes.

Scope: The list of all the items included as part of the project.

Skeuomorphism: The process of making web items resemble real-world items to help people connect the digital to the real world.

SMART Goals: Goals that are Specific, Measurable, Attainable, Relevant, and Time-specific.

Software: The programs and other operating information used by a computer.

Specialized interface: An interface that has unique patterns and interactions not commonly used in most products, whether it is a unique variation on an existing interface or a new interface that must be designed from scratch.

Stakeholder/Decision maker: A person with an interest or concern in something, especially a business. Often a boss or someone with power to change the direction or cancel a project.

Success: The accomplishment of an aim or purpose.

SWOT analysis: SWOT stands for Strengths, Weaknesses, Opportunities, and Threats. SWOT analysis is a method of identifying each of those factors for your business.

Takeaway: A key fact, point, or idea to be remembered, typically one emerging from a discussion or meeting.

Target audience: a particular group at which a product is aimed.

Testing scenario: A detailed story that provides context for a testing task.

Testing task: A task that test participants will be asked to complete in a product.

Traffic: The number of visitors to a site.

User Interface (UI): The means by which the user and a computer system interact, in particular the use of input devices and software.

Usability report: A document that summaries the degree to which a product is able be used, as well as recommendations for improvement.

User experience: The overall experience of a person using a product such as a website or computer application, especially in terms of how easy or pleasing it is to use.

User goals: A final state which user strives. To get the goal, a user may perform multiple steps or tasks.

User research: Multiple methods of obtaining information and feedback from users or potential users.

User-centered Design: A framework of processes (not restricted to interfaces or technologies) in which usability goals, user characteristics, environment, tasks and workflow of a product, service or process are given extensive attention at each stage of the design process.

Validation: The action of checking or proving the validity or accuracy of something.

Value proposition: An innovation, service, or feature intended to make a company or product attractive to customers.

Vision statement: The method a company will use to achieve it's mission.

Voice and tone: Refers to the writing and communication attributes of your brand.

Website: A location connected to the Internet that maintains one or more pages on the World Wide Web.

Wireframe: A page schematic or screen blueprint. It is a visual guide that represents the skeletal framework of a website.

Zombie apps: Products or apps that are unfindable by any means except searching directly by name. Products or apps that have never been downloaded or have less than 50 downloads.

Acknowledgments

This book.
We can't believe it's done.

Reflecting on the long, rarely glorious journey, it's so clear that this book is so much more than simply the product of our writing. At each step, the support, feedback and contributions of so many people have made this possible and, while we can't thank them enough, we'd like to try here.

Our deepest thanks to:

Deb Hardy, truly one of the best editors around. Your developmental edits played a monumental role in the shape of this book and can't be overstated. Thank you so much for pushing us to create the book we have today. You're amazing.

Meg Foley, an exceptional editor and manager. Despite the odds, you took this book from start to finish with us, improving it at each step. Thanks for getting us over the finish line, and for being so committed to seeing this through.

Michelle Sanchez, who breathes life into brands across the web. Your designs made it real in a way that it hadn't felt to that point. Thank you for bringing our vision to life on the page. It exceeds expectation.

Sarah Doody, who stepped in and joined our book adventure without a second thought. You really got our vision for the book and your foreword is perfect. Thank you for being a part of this.

Our amazing team of content readers, including: Rebecca Blakison, Alice Reyzin, Erika Lee, Cara Nelson, Jim O'Neill, Juhan Sohin, Angelia Baxter, and Ehi Aimiuwu. Your suggestions, insights and questions led us to creating a book that made sense and flowed better. Thank you.

Dave Gray, who kindly lent us use of his Empathy Map.

Chanaye Thomas, who delivered a timely and well considered SWOT analysis on the Pixels for Humans social feeds.

The folks at O'Reilly who's initial interest in this topic led to our first draft and got us started.

Jen's Harvard Extension class *Planning Successful Websites and Apps* of 2014 who were the first recipients of this book's contents, in lecture format. Thank you for working through the material in its rawest state. Because of you, we saw the potential for writing this book and were able to adapt it from presentation to page.

All the folks who've supported and encouraged us to continue along the way.

Also Jen says...

To Heather. The book wouldn't exist without you, full stop. Thank you for all of your efforts to get it into this final format, published, and existing. What are we making next? :-D

And **to all of my students** through the years, especially the Digital Media Design students at Harvard University Extension School, this book is for you. This is the material that sets you apart from everyone else in your field. Start with these principles and this process, apply those marvelous critical thinking skills of yours, and create something amazing. As always, I can't wait to see what you make next!

And finally, Heather says...

There are so many people in my life who've shaped who I am and what I do (including writing this book). And I'm so grateful for each and every one of them.

First, to one of the best people in tech and my mentor, coach and friend, **Whitney Hess**: thank you. You believed in me before I did and helped me find the perspective I needed to keep going. From the depths of my heart, thank you.

To my brilliant and wonderful co-author, **Jen Kramer.** I'm so grateful for you, your work, and your friendship. Here's to many more collaborations and good times.

To colleagues, friends, and peers who make tech a joy to be a part of: Hana Zaydens, Kevin Grinberg, Lis Hubert, Steve Krug, Rebecca Blakison, Pam Drouin, Lisa Maria Martin, Eryn O'Neil, Audra Congress, C. Todd Lombardo, Malaika Carpenter, Ehi Aimiuwu, B. Cordelia Yu, Angelia Baxter, Leo Gomez Blum, Maureen Barlow, Matt DiGirolamo, Abhishek Murali Iyengar, Kirsten Lindquist Campana, Andrew Maier, Kyle Soucy, Susan Mercer, and Stevie T. A. Nguyen. Each of you makes my life and my work that much better by being in it.

To **Juhan Sohin**, who has welcomed me at every turn with open arms, support and kindness. Your work in the industry is so valuable and I'm grateful to call you friend.

To **Alice Reyzin, Michelle Sanchez, Elle Elliott, Katelyn Valentine, Ada Powers,** and **Opeola Bukola**, some of my all-time favorite people. Your friendship is invaluable and a beacon in my life.

To my business besties, without whom I wouldn't have the thriving business I have today: Jeannie Sullivan, Naliah Blades, Colleen O'Connor, Lindsey Liu, Leah Neaderthal, Jasmine Shea, Lisa Goldstein Graham, Megan Flatt, Ticora Davis, Alfredo Gutierrez, Deb Hardy, and Stephanie Berchiolly. Your insights and support are always on point and I'm grateful for the opportunity to grow my business alongside yours.

To my Pixels for Humans team past, present and future, including Chanaye Thomas, Asa Todd, Lanya Olmsted, Nick Clark, Katie Zenger, Amy Caffee, and Tori Dunlap. I know you'll all kick butt in everything you do, and I'm grateful to be a part of your journey.

To my supportive family, with a big shout out to my mom and siblings who are always ready to dive in to whatever wild adventure I've got in mind. Thanks for encouraging me to always be me.

To that dude I met playing ultimate in January 2008. A decade of knowing you and 8 years of marriage later, things aren't too bad. Here's to 80 more. <3

To Rebekah. You are the highlight of my life and I'm grateful every day that you call me 'Mama'. I love you.

Jen Kramer

For nearly twenty years, Jen Kramer has been educating clients, colleagues, friends and graduate students about the meaning of a "quality website."

Since 2000, she has built websites that are supportive of business and marketing goals in a freelance capacity and as part of an agency.

Jen is a Lecturer at Harvard University Extension School in the Master's of Liberal Arts in Digital Media Design, teaching at least five courses per year, advising students, and assisting in curriculum design. She is a 2018 Petra Shattuck Award winner, presented for excellence in teaching.

Jen is also a prolific video author, creating over 35 training courses for Lynda.com (a division of LinkedIn Learning), O'Reilly Media, Aquent Gymnasium, osTraining, and Frontend Masters.

Before You Code is her third book. Previous titles include Joomla Start to Finish (2010) and Joomla 24-Hour Trainer (2011).

Jen is also available for individual private tutoring, customized classroom training, and occasional freelance web design work.

Jen earned a BS in biology at University of North Carolina at Chapel Hill and an MS in Internet Strategy Management at the Marlboro College Graduate School.

Heather O'Neill

Heather O'Neill is a product strategist and SaaS business consultant with over a decade of experience creating meaningful products for the people who use them.

At Pixels for Humans, Heather helps SaaS start-ups solve their toughest challenges and grow into mature, community-focused businesses, that center people over profits.

A problem solver at heart, Heather also works with design teams to define problems, hypothesize solutions, and track success in their work. Heather has taught classes and workshops at Harvard Extension School, O'Reilly, UXPA International, and more.

Heather is also the author of several video courses including Measured UX, her signature course for UX designers. The course trains designers on how to collect, refine, and analyze quantitative data as part of a UX design process. Students finish the course able to solve problems more effectively and track the impact of their design iterations.

Heather is the 2018 recipient of Rhode Island's Tech10 Women in Tech award. She earned a dual BA in mathematics and music at Northeastern University in Boston, graduating Cum Laude in 2006.

At Pixels we believe that technology can make the world a better place for everyone. To get there, we work with SaaS startups to create intentional businesses that care – about their impact on individuals, society and the world. Pixels for Humans was founded in 2014 and is headquartered in the Greater Boston Area, serving clients globally.